Speedway Kings

of Southwestern Pennsylvania & Region

100 Years of Racing History

Marci Lynn McGuinness

Speedway Kings of Southwestern Pennsylvania,
100 Years of Racing History
© Marci Lynn McGuinness 2011

ISBN 13: 978-0-938833-42-0
Printed in the U.S.A.

Order autographed books at $34.95per copy. Free shipping.
Request bulk prices or schedule a speaking engagement.
Shore Publications, P. O. Box 987, Hopwood, PA 15445
724-710-2919   shorepublications@yahoo.com

Printable order forms and online ordering: www.uniontownspeedway.com; www.ohiopyle.info

A special thanks to Brynn Cunningham for editing the board track section of this book.

Front Cover Photographs: L.J. Dennis is in the dust behind car #5!
Back Cover Black & White Photographs: Top photo – Uniontown Speedway board track curves were banked at 34 degrees. The the tunnel (left) spectators took from the infield to the grandstands (far left) from 1916 to 1922.
Bottom photo: Louis Chevrolet and Fred Duesenberg are shoulder to shoulder, center in suits, at the last race at the Uniontown Speedway board track, 1922. August Duesenberg, second from right. Driver, Ralph Mulford, right of Fred. The Chevrolets and Duesenbergs attended every race here. Louis won the first Universal Films Trophy. These men owned many of the cars on the track. Chevrolet's race cars were Frontenacs.

DARK PHOTO NOTE: Several news articles and photographs appear dark in this book. This is due to their aged, dark and crumbling conditions. I felt it more important to include the historical information rather than let it turn to dust and lose it forever.

Contents

Dedication

Emedio Guerrieri was 16 years old when he went to the first board track race at the Uniontown Speeway. He took most of the photographs in the first half of this book, keeping a chronological album. Guerrieri photographed each race through 1922. Recently, his daughter found the album in his cedar chest, which had not been opened since his death in 1950.
It is due to his neice, Filomena Glad, that I am able to share the 100 historical photographs of these famous men and time.

When asked to write about my grandfather, Emedio Guerrieri, I was unsure of what to write. He had died in 1952 when I was only two years old. His widow, Helen, my much loved grandmother, lived another forty-six years, so I decided to draw on her thoughts and memories.

  Emedio Guerrieri was born in Rome, Italy, in 1900. As an infant, he and his mother, Adele Guerrieri, emigrated to the United States and settled in Uniontown, Pennsylvania. Here they joined husband and father, John Guerrieri, who had emigrated earlier. The family settled in Uniontown because it reminded John of his home in the Abruzzi Region of Italy. They had five more children and lived the rest of their lives there.

  John and Adele's first child, Emedio, graduated from Uniontown High School on June 11, 1918. He was Valedictorian of his class. His Valedictorian speech was entitled: "It's Fundamental Value to Liberty," pertaining to the flag of the United States and WW I. His senior quote was, "A kind true heart, a spirit high, that could not fear and would not bow, were written in his manly eyes and in his manly brow." Author unknown.

Emedio Guerrieri (left in WWI uniform) was 16 years old when the Uniontown Speedway board track opened its box office. It must have been pain-staking work to take the 125 photos found in his album. He was a student at the time, 16 to 22 years of age as the track went on. He did not realize this collection would find its way into a book on the region's racing history. Helen Guerrieri, right, shown here, peeks out of the corn where she was hiding from her future husband.

  Emedio married Helen Rotunno of Morgantown, West Virginia, after graduating from the School of Pharmacy at West Virginia University. They had two children, the late Professor Kathleen G. Rousseau of Morgantown, and the late Dr. Emedio B. Guerrieri of Escondido, California.

  Emedio and Helen were devoted to their family and community. In his early years at WVU, Emedio took many photographs of the campus and marching drill teams of the WW I soldiers. After his marriage he took photographs of their travels. My beloved grandmother saved and cherished these photographs. After her death in 1998 and the death of my mother in 1999, I had the opportunity to go through these old photos. They were thrilling to see. One was of General ' Black Jack' Pershing riding his horse down Main Street in Uniontown. I framed it and gave it to my son-in-law, Lt. Col. EJ Dupont, who is in the Army. There were many lovely photos of my grandmother and their children, family, friends, and neighbors.

John and Adele Guerrieri's youngest daughter, Frances Guerrieri, married Amadee Gismondi, and they made their home in Uniontown. This lovely couple had two daughters, Filomena and Adele Gismondi. These pretty girls married young men from Uniontown. Filomena married the late Jerome Glad. They had two sons, the late Bernie Glad and Dr. Lawrence Glad. Adele Gismondi would marry Steven Kezmarsky. They had two sons, Stephen Kezmarsky, Jr. and Robert Kezmarsky. The family continues to grow...and to love and appreciate their roots in beautiful Western Pennsylvania.

When I came across the photo album of the old race track in Uniontown, I recalled the story my grandmother often told. She and her husband loved the races and went often. She always spoke of having the privilege of seeing Barney Oldfield race. I decided to give the album to my cousin, Filomena Glad. She also cherishes her family and loves the history of family and of Uniontown. Filomena shared this photo album and hence the photographs for this book.

It is a great joy to know that quite often preservation of even the smallest kind can bring happiness and excitement to people. Nothing would make my grandparents happier than knowing that their love and memories are still being enjoyed. Thank you.

Sincerely,
Victoria E. Warner

This book is in memory of the late Bernie Glad.

Acknowledgements

It has been 17 years since the late Jim Boyd of Jockey Hollow, Pennsylvania, called and invited me to see his collection of Uniontown Speedway board track photographs. He stood there in his basement with a smile, arms overflowing, and made me promise to "do something" with the lost history of the race track that made Uniontown nationally famous from 1916 – 1922.

Two years later, in 1996, I published the book *Yesteryear at the Uniontown Speedway*. Eighty photographs and information from the old newspapers and race programs take readers to a day when the heroes and gentlemen of the industrial revolution made history here. The book is in its third edition, thanks to the Summit Inn who sponsored it, and I have written a screenplay, *Speed Kings*, about the story and characters behind the wildcat track. Through the years, I have pieced together the relationships between track sponsors such as the President of Universal Films, Carl Laemmle, Silent Film Star Vivian Prescott and her husband, who was Manager of Events and Flagman, Uniontown's George Titlow, coal barons and more.

Uniontown was the wealthiest town in America, and the rich played here as early drivers set speed records and entertained crowds of up to 50,000 spectators. In the fifteen years since publishing *Yesteryear at the Uniontown Speedway*, I have come to understand the rise and fall of our board track and its patrons.

There are three people who initially encouraged me to write another book on our area's racing story. They are: Jimmy Shaffer of Shaffer's Towing in Masontown, Lou Ansel of Ansel's Tire Outlet in McClellandtown, and Filomena Glad, who called when her great uncle's collection of board track photographs were discovered. A big thanks to them for giving me the push I needed.

There are two men who taught me what I know about cars. They are the late Jimmy Bendishaw of Hopwood and John Wingard of Ohiopyle. Many thanks to them both for the laughter, stories, assistance, memories, and education.

No one was more excited than Jimmy when I published that first book. He actually giggled when I handed him his autographed copy in the living room of his Meadowbrook home, just steps from the old track. That giggle rings in my ears this day. And Jim Boyd was relieved. He died in his slep not long after its publication.

John Wingard is a man of great patience and ingenuity without whom my daughters' cars would never have made it over the mountain and back during high school. Thanks, Wing Nut!

During the organization of *Speedway Kings of Southwestern Pennsylvania & Region*, 100 Years of Racing History, I interviewed race car drivers, historians, enthusiasts, and their loved ones. Their contributions of time, stories, photographs, albums, news articles, and energy have enabled me to preserve this representation of our area's contribution to the beloved sport of auto racing, from 1903 through 2011.

Many thanks to the contributors and sponsors without whom this book would not have been produced:

Contributors: Lou Ansel, Bob Arsenberger, Larry Baker, Steve Baker, Jimmy, Jr., Josh and Pam Bendishaw, Stacey Bortz, Bud Bradmon, Loretta Buterbaugh, Jim Campbell, Ernie Cerini, Bud Cryster, Gregg Dahl, L. J. Dennis, Alan Detweiller, Bob Falcon, Filomena Glad, Dirt Henry, Dale Holder, Billy Horner, Dave Kittey, Bobby Lake, Patty Leighgabor, Richard Macaladi, Mel Minnick, Jr., Kenny Mitchell, Russ Redshaw, Mark Richards, Jr., Jack Ruckus, Dick Rugh, Peggy Schultz, Bill Scott, Jimmy Shaffer, Lyndal Shaw, Garry Sisson, Dana Whipkey, Rhonda Zeigler.

Introduction

In the early days of automobiles, film, and the industrial revolution, southwestern Pennsylvania's coal and coke boom attracted the major businessmen and celebrities of our country. It has been my great privilege to piece together some of their associations and involvements with the Uniontown Speedway board track's organization, rein, and demise. For instance:

Edwin Porter was born in Connellsville. He worked for **Thomas Edison**, operating camera equipment, directing silent film actors, and creating short films. He directed *The Great Train Robbery* in 1903. It was billed as the main attraction at the country's first **nickelodeon** in 1905. This western's success solidified motion pictures as commercial entertainment in America.

Henry Ford also worked for **Thomas Edison** at this time. He soon resigned because he focused too much on his own automobile production interests. They remained very close friends throughout their lives. They were also friends with **Harvey Firestone,** who supplied tires for Ford**.** In 1902, Ford hired bicycle racer Barney Oldfield to promote his new car using Firestone Tires. Ford was backing Oldfield when he raced at Pittsburgh's Brunot's Island Raceway in 1905.

Harvey Firestone – In 1895, Henry Ford walked into Firestone's shop, contracted him to make tires for his autos, and changed the industries forever. Ford was sponsoring Oldfield when he raced at the Brunot Island Race Track in Pittsburgh in1905, three years after Titlow brought the first car to Uniontown. Firestone sponsored the Summit Mountain Hill Climbs from 1913 – 1915 - a direct result of George Titlow's acquaintance with him and his cronies. In 1918, he created the tough Oldfield Tire to ward against the damage of splinters from board track racing. All racecars used this tire, saving them many tire changes and enabling them to drive faster. Oldfield's slogan was, "The only insurance I need is Oldfield Tires."

Rockwell and Marcus Marietta – The Marietta brothers were the middle children of 19. They ran Connellsville during the coal and coke boom. Rockwell became its first mayor after serving on the council for many years. Their sister was town treasurer. A few of their businesses were: The Yough Hotel, The Marietta Hotel, Connellsville Brewing Company, and the Uniontown Brewing Company. Their hotels were located adjacent to the railroad station and housed wealthy travelers at a time when Connellsville was a rich, bustling hub. In 1886, they hired George Flavius Titlow as a clerk at their Yough Hotel. Titlow had a lot of personality, and the Marietta's needed a man whom their rich clients would enjoy and trust.

George Flavius Titlow - George Flavius Titlow grew up in Uniontown, Pennsylvania. He worked at his father's tailor shop and department store in downtown Uniontown for four years after graduating from high school. In 1886, he took a job as clerk at the Yough House Hotel in nearby Connellsville. Hotel owners Rockwell and Marcus Marietta owned the bustling enterprise and were instrumental in running the wealthy town during the coal and coke boom.

   In 1888, the Mariettas built the Marietta Hotel and promoted Titlow to manage the new establishment. Titlow had caught onto the hotel business quickly. His flamboyant, likeable personality and intelligence endeared him to the important businessmen he met every day.
By 1890, George Titlow was married and owned his own hotel, the Jennings House, in downtown Uniontown. Here, Titlow thrived while Uniontown joined the coal and coke boom. In 1902, when there were 5,000 automobiles in America, George Titlow was among those car owners, the only one in Uniontown. He then proceeded to bring auto racing, film stars and glamour to Fayette County.

Henry Frick – Coal and Coke Baron extraordinaire. Frick was a fierce businessman who helped bring down J.V. Thompson and associates.

J.V. Thompson – Coal Baron and President of the First National Bank in downtown Uniontown. J.V. bought and sold hundreds of millions of dollars worth of coal lands, amassing a fortune for himself and many others. When his wife passed away he married an actress. Her lifestyle and the 1913 divorce cost him a large part of his fortune. He became land poor. Frick bought his coal properties for a pittance, after which he spiraled from immense wealthy into poverty. It was 1915, when internationally famous drivers, and pioneers of the industrial and motion picture revolutions were in town. It is a shame he could not have enjoyed that time in style. George Titlow had campaigned for Thompson for Governor in 1906, when J.V. was on top of the world.

Charlie Johnson – Early Uniontown Speed King and garage owner. His Standard Garage was located behind the Titlow Hotel at the corner of Peter and Arch Streets. In 1915, Johnson beat Ralph DePalma during the third annual Summit Mountain Hill Climb just after DePalma had won the Indianapolis 500. Johnson raced bicycles before cars. He was acclaimed as President of the Uniontown Speedway Association until absconding to Cuba with the proceeds in 1922.

Carl Laemmle – Universal Films President and friend of Thomas Edison and Henry Ford. The year after he opened his Universal Film Studios in Hollywood, he sponsored the Universal Films Trophy for the annual Universal Films Race at the Uniontown Speedway board track. During the track's rein, Universal was the largest and most famous film company in the world. After beating Edison in court, fighting for the right to be an independent film company, the men became friends. Universal Films filmed every race at the Uniontown track, playing the movies each year at local theatres before and after the races. The Universal Films Trophy was handed down to the winner of the big race each year. Jimmy Murphy won it in 1922 in the same Duesenberg #12 that he won the Indy 500 and Gran Prix in that year.

Barney Oldfield – In 1902, Henry Ford hired Barney Oldfield (World's most famous race car driver) to ride around the country in his FORD® promoting the automobiles. These men made each other a household name. Oldfield had been a bicycle racer. He had the first race car with a roof built, the Golden Submarine, in 1918. Oldfield was also a film star. He became such a draw that he was paid $4,000 for speaking engagements, and $1,000 just for showing up at a race.

Vivian Prescott – Prescott was the most famous silent film star of the day and never missed a race at the Uniontown Speedway board track. Her husband, Neil Whalen, was Manager of Events and Flagman at the track. He had been a racecar driver and owned a large New York automobile dealership. Prescott starred in 202 silent films. She was the first woman to drive on the Indianapolis Race Track.

Louis Chevrolet – Louis started out by racing bicycles. He built a Frontenac bike and later used the name for his race cars. He met Willie Vanderbilt in Europe while repairing the millionaire auto racer's bike. Vanderbilt recognized Chevrolet's talents and invited him to America, but he did not move at that time. In 1905, while working for Manhatten Fiat, he began racing, setting records, and repeatedly beating Barney Oldfield. He beat Oldfield 10 out of 11 races at Brunots Island Raceway in Pittsburgh that year, winning AAA Champion Car for the season. Louis Chevrolet and his brothers built the Frontenac race car, which won many a race in Uniontown. He won the first Universal Films Trophy in 1916 as driver.

Fred and August Duesenberg – In 1919 one of Duesenbergs star drivers, Tommy Milton, set 19 new speed records for distances up to 300 miles with a 16-valve "Duesie" racing engine. That same year the "Duesie" race car team of Murphy and Milton set 52 AAA records on the Uniontown boards. In **1920** Duesenberg Automobiles and Motors was formed. Five months later, they started another company just for their racing activities. The company was called Duesenberg Brothers, and it achieved considerable glory in the following seven years. Their 183 cid straight-eight race car started winning right away in 1920 with top drivers like Jimmy Murphy and Tommy Milton.

In 1932, ten years after the track closed, Fred Duesenberg died from complications after a crash, speeding and testing the brakes in a new car along Lincoln Highway near the Jennerstown Speedway. The Duesenberg brothers attended every race here, as they rose in prominence in their field.

Pioneer Auto Racing in SW PA, 1903 – 1915

Brunot Island Race Track was a one-mile dirt oval that ran from 1903 to 1914. It began as a horse racing track. The island sits in the Ohio River just west of Pittsburgh in Allegheny County. The first year that Louis Chevrolet raced, 1905, he beat Barney Oldfield in 10 out of 11 races here, winning AAA Champion Car for the season.

   In 1906, George Titlow built the plushest hotel in western Pennsylvania. The Titlow Hotel was headquarters for coal, coke, and steel barons through 1922. He also entertained five governors, film stars, race car drivers, high powered hoteliers, and the like. This same year, his friend, District Attorney William Crow, became Senator, Titlow campaigned for J.V. Thompson for Governor, Coal Baron James Barnes built the Barnes Estate in Hopwood, and Barney Oldfield starred in the Broadway show, *The Vanderbilt Cup*. Barnes traveled to New York City often to entertain wealthy customers of the First National Bank. Fifteen hundred attended the grand opening at the elegant Titlow Hotel, filling Uniontown's downtown from sun up to the wee hours.

   In 1912, George Titlow served as Entertainment Chairman during Uniontown's "Old Home Week" celebration. He set up a dirt track for auto racing. Charlie Johnson raced there. This track was a real hit, which prompted Titlow to start the first Fayette Auto Club and Summit Mountain Hill Climb.

In 1914, professional drivers came to Uniontown for the second annual hill climb, which was sponsored by Firestone Tires. This was the last year for races at Brunot's Island Raceway in Pittsburgh, and the beginning of national fame and fortune for Uniontown. Motorcycles raced this year, causing extreme excitement. George Titlow was speaking with Dr. Joseph Van Kirk outside the Summit Hotel when the doctor fell dead from the excitement and heat. Titlow's Peerless car caught on fire twice this day.

George Flavius Titlow set auto racing in motion in Uniontown, PA.

Left: In 1914, the only motorcycle to make it to the top of Summit Mountain was driven by Homer Mathis of Charleroi. I believe this is his Flying Merkle.
Right: 1914 Summit Mountain Hill Climb. The Summit Hotel sits to the left. The banner says, "Firestone Tires."

George Flavius Titlow is standing behind the car in the center with a cap and bow tie. His son has his arm over his shoulder. The building to the left is the Mountain Water Club. It stood half way up Summit Mountain at the watering trough. A few men seem to be security or law enforcement.
In 1914 and 1915, they set up the hill climb announcer's station there. The sign on the pole to Titlow's left says "Go to Stone House." Titlow bought the Fayette Springs Hotel in 1909, added the front rooms, and named it the Stone House. It was his family's weekend and summer home, just east of Chalk Hill on the National Road. Was he inviting the 4,000 Summit Mountain Hill Climb spectators to an after-race party? I think Rockwell Marietta is the man standing in the back of the car on the right with his brother, Marcus, next to him.

The Mountain Water Club, Summit Mountain Hill Climb, 1915. George Titlow (second to the right on porch) and friends. The tables are set up for the announcer and score keepers. Is that a cooker to the right? Notice the man with an apron and chef's hat to the left of the cooker.

In 1915, Charlie Johnson, Uniontown's own Speed King and owner of the Standard Garage at Arch and Peter Streets, beat Indy 500 winner Ralph DePalma at the Summit Mountain Hill Climb race. Johnson quit driving after that but built several cars and sponsored other drivers. When Ed Shaffer died in George Titlow's arms because of a crash caused by a misunderstood AAA flag, Johnson talked against Titlow, who had mentored him for many years. Titlow wanted the AAA to take responsibility, but Johnson saw an opening for him to become Speed King, and he grabbed that flag, changing their relationship for the rest of their lives.

Summit Mountain heading west, 1915. Notice the billboards near the Mountain Water Club.

1915 - All these bikes are Harley Davidson® motorcycles except the one to the far left. What is it? They may be preparing for a Hill Climb. This is in Uniontown. Can you identify the location?

Uniontown Speedway Board Track, 1916

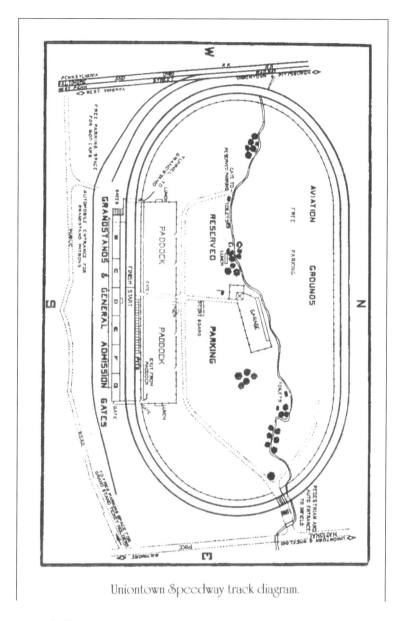

Uniontown Speedway track diagram.

Uniontown Speedway track diagram. Notice the creek running through the infield. This stream runs along the Adrian's Market parking lot in Hopwood. The track was a 1 1/8 mile oval, built of Hemlock 2 x 4's laid together face to face. It was enormous, running from the National Road to the railroad tracks. Kenny Mitchell said, "The wood was grooved, to help it fit together." This track was a national destination and took up a large part of Hopwood for seven years.

1916 was a very big year for Uniontown. Five days before the fourth annual Summit Mountain Hill Climb, the Pennsylvania Highway Department outlawed the races. This prompted Charlie Johnson to contact Jack Prince. Jack and Charlie had both been bicycle racers, as had Chevrolet, Oldfield and many others. Prince was building and promoting wooden race tracks at this time. Johnson formed the Uniontown Speedway Association, was voted in as President, and raised funds to construct a 1 1/8 mile board track in Hopwood, Pennsylvania. This track was faster than Indianapolis, had 34 degree banked curves, drew crowds of up to 50,000 spectators, and attracted the best drivers in the world. The land was leased from the Brownfields.

Charlie Johnson stands in the front of this shot with a cigar in his left hand, during the construction of the Uniontown Speedway board track, November 1916.

16

Unloading wood from the train. The American Lumber Company in Pittsburgh supplied the lumber required to build this track, 1916.

Uniontown Speedway board track under construction, 1916. Workers completed the track in two months time! There were no wood screws then. It took a few nails to withstand automobiles flying at over 100 mile per hour for seven years.

This photo shows the grandstand to the left with the tunnel (center) that spectators took from the infield (right) to their seats. Is the mechanic standing up in the front car to the right?

This *Pittsburgh Sunday Leader* newspaper article tells the story of the tragedy that took five lives and injured 17 at the Uniontown Speedway's Preliminary Opening Race on December 2, 1916. Article date is December 3, 1916.

THE WEATHER
PROBABLY LOCAL RAINS TO-
NIGHT TUESDAY PROBABLY
CLOUDY AND CONTINUED
WARM
HIGH WATER MARK 23,979.

Daily Ne

THE ONLY DEMOCR

VOL. 21, NO. 110.

UNIONTO

FRANK GALVIN DIED AT 11:40; SPEEDWAY DEAD REACHES FIVE

LOCK
FOR
TH

**MAN WHO DROVE DEATH CAR ON-
LY SPOKE TWICE SINCE SAT-
URDAY'S DREADFUL
ACCIDENT**

ONE OF BEST IN THE GAME

**NEARLY DEAD ONCE BEFORE—
WORE A PLATE IN SKULL AS
MEMENTO OF FORMER ACCI-
DENT—SWEETHEART WITH HIM
WHEN HE DIED.**

Frank Galvin, driver of the death car at Sunbury races, passed away in a private home at the Uniontown hospital this morning at 11 P. M. By his side was Miss Lillian Shafer of Indianapolis, his sweetheart, who had traveled from her home to watch Galvin send his Premier across the line a winner in the Universal classic.

FETTERMAN SHOWS NERVE

L. I. (Ike) Fetterman, of Pittsburgh, one of the best known drivers in the races last Saturday showed remarkable nerve when he piloted the Peerless car about the speedway for the last 25 miles at the 50-mile Peerless race after a sudden epileptic fit became imbedded in his left eye.

On the 75th lap, just as he passed the leading Haynes car in a split he never knew from any of the rest of the Peerless race driver's nervous system did not permit knowledge of the incident until the conclusion of the race. Fetterman was taken to a local hotel and as a result of careful attention unable to be out today.

WANTED

Final Editions of Saturday's issue (December 2, 1916) of the News Standard. Will pay five cents cash for copies in good condition. Mail or send to News Standard Business Office.

WHO PLACED STRYCHNINE IN THE BOTTLE?

POISONING OF MRS. ELBA MAHA-
NEY DEVELOPS INTO A DEEP
MYSTERY OF THE COURT
HOUSE

CONGRESS TAKES UP PROBLEM OF LIVING COSTS

(By United Press.)
Washington, D. C., Dec. 11—Legislative proposals intended to curtail the high cost of living marked the opening of Congress today.

Representative Fitzgerald, leader of the majority forces introduced two plans, two of them to call for the reduction of cold storage and the division of control over country on food.

Representatives Fitzgerald was prepared as chairman of the committee and Representative Lever of New York, a Socialist, backed on a number tax measure to control the distribution.

Co-operation from industrial is not again the open contract law.

HAD HARD FIGHT FOR LIFE

Strychnine is believed to have been placed in the brown effect bottle from which Mrs. Elba Mahaney was poisoned tablets were poisoned a dose of strychnine at the court house. Strychnine in each cell in the bottle's contents was not such word. Mrs. Mahaney's case was discovered as strychnine following and only was treated accordingly and...

RUNAWA
UCED T
REA

CAR GOT H

CHURCH
ARE R

21

Continued from First Page.

Chevrolet Is Prize Winner

Chevrolet took the lead for the remaining 38 laps of the race.

The Official Results.

The winners in the Universal trophy contest follow:

First—Louis Chevrolet, Frontenac car, prize $1,000. Time, 1 hour, 14 minutes and 12½ seconds.

Second—Dave Lewis, Premier car, prize $700. Time—1 hour, 16 minutes and 36 1-5 seconds.

Third—Ralph De Palma, Mercedes car, prize $500. Time—1 hour, 17 minutes and 56 1-5 seconds.

Fourth—Barney Newgard, Crawford car, prize $400. Time—1 hour and 25 minutes flat.

Fifth—Milt McBride, Olsen car, prize $300. Time—1 hour, 25 minutes and 18 seconds.

Other Starters in Race.

Other starters for the Universal trophy contest were: Ira Vail, Hudson; John De Palma, J. J. R. Special; Arthur Klein, Crawford; Frank Galvin, Premier; Charley Devlin, Dusenberg; Jimmy Benedict, Blue Bird; Bert Watson, Olsen; George Buzano, Dusenberg; George Adams, Adams Special; James Meyers, Pugh Special; Otto Henning, Ogren; Hugo Ogren, Ogren, and Jack Gable, Burman Peugeot.

The results in the dealers' race were:

First—L. I. Fetterman, Peerless car, prize $500. Time, 50 minutes and 44 seconds.

Second—F. M. McCarthy, prize $300.

Third—H. L. Robinson, prize $200.

Frank Galvin Died

Continued from First Page.

new drivers looked for are Dario Resta, Johnny Aitken, Earl Cooper, Eddie Rickenbacker, Eddie Pullen, together with all of the present race, if they are living.

The body of Hughie Hughes was shipped forward to Los Angeles Monday afternoon. Friends of the dead driver in Los Angeles including Frank Lowry, a race track promoter, and Earl Cooper, prominent driver, will look after the arrangements for Mrs. Hughes, the widow.

Remains of Gaston Weigle, Galvin's mechanician on the Premier death messenger, went forward to Indianapolis, his home, Sunday afternoon at 4:20. The body was accompanied by a half dozen friends of the little racer.

GETTING READY FOR MORE.

As shock of the death blow rendered Saturday afternoon by the 1,800 pound runaway Premier subsides, current thought runs to the next races of the local Speedway, despite its costly baptism of blood at the initial opening. Officials who have acted at a score of like events pronounce the local track on a par with the fastest, and declare at completion it will be one of the few perfect motor racing equipments in the country.

Never had a prettier race been run than up to the 45th lap, when Hughes experienced his first tire trouble. Almost wheel to wheel Hughes, Chevrolet and DePalma circled the saucer, with the Englishman and Frenchman alternating at setting the pace.

Seldom do drivers pay attention to the momentary lead during a long race. Every thought is devoted to conserving the machine so that it can endure the test and at the same time produce the best results. For this reason a lap counts nothing, if the extra speed necessary to gain the lap forces the leader to wear his car out before the race is run.

Out to win, Hughes by his happy disposition and inclination to inject a thrill by a display of speed at the turns, was easily the idol of the crowd. When Fetterman in his Peerless cleared the track after making the round as pacemaker for the first lap, Hughes opened his red flyer up and was away to a lead, which many believe would have ended with his victory.

Chevrolet, sticking close to the middle of the track, hugged the Hoosine, never deviating and never increasing or reducing his speed, which he kept at 90 miles an hour as the cars flew around the track.

Where Saturday's Awful Accident Occurred

This December 4, 1916, article is from Uniontown's *Daily News Standard,* but I could not get the last few paragraphs scanned. They describe the details of the crash, which was gory. The Universal Films camera-man insisted on filming and got thrown out. He did return, but it is said that the films were destroyed.

press on the inside.

Hughes tried the latter, sweeping down the curve, smashing through the guard rail with his brakes on. Both Hughes and his mechanician, Russell Burns, of Chicago, were well protected beneath the steel slip in the event the car overturned. The sturdy machine flung itself around in a circle three times, knocking down stakes and sending flying chips of wood right and left. It halted right side up.

CHEERS TURN TO HORROR.

With cheers ringing in his ears from all sides, Hughes and Burns proceeded around to the front of the track where hundreds awaited in anxiety to learn the result of the accident. Word had spread that the Hoskins was caught and when Hughes in his green knickerbocker suit walked before the press box uninjured he was enthusiastically received.

The cars were speeding on the last half of the race and Hughes stopped to shake the hand of J. C. Hoskins, owner of the car, when the odd twist of destiny loomed up in the shape of Frank Galvin's Premier. Hoskins flung himself flat to one side. A second before he had felt the warm grip of his driver's hand.

Then the uninjured and first aid men began to succor the wounded. Up in the far end of the field, the band, ignorant of the accident, was playing a happy tune, while the drivers, unaware of the seriousness of the affair, increased their speed if anything, as the race neared the finished.

THE RESULTS.

The time and order in which the racers finished was as follows:

First—Louis Chevrolet, Frontenac car, prize $1,000. Time, 1 hour, 14 minutes and 12 2-5 seconds.

Second—Dave Lewis, Premier car, prize, $700. Time 1 hour, 16 minutes and 36 1-5 seconds.

Third—Ralph DePalma, Mercedes car, prize $500. Time, 1 hour, 17 minutes and 56 2-5 seconds.

Fourth—Barney Newgard, Crawford car, prize $400. Time, 1 hour and 25 minutes flat.

Fifth—Milt McBride, Olsen car, prize $300. Time, 1 hour, 25 minutes.

Ten minutes after the Universal classic, the five remaining cars in the dealer's race were pushed on the track and the second event was on. I. P. Fetterman of Pittsburgh, a local favorite, in his green Peerless, won the race through plucky driving and avoidance of any tire trouble. Until the last five laps he trailed the Murray Special, driven by Fred McCarthy. In the last six miles he added ten miles an hour to his running time and could not be headed by the Murray. Fetterman averaged 80 miles an hour. McCarthy in the Murray finished second and H. L. Robinson in the Haynes took third money.

BURNING OF THE HAYNES.

The spectacular feature of this race was the burning of the Haynes No. 9, driven by J. E. Conway. On the south bank the Haynes caught fire and Conway stopped his car several hundred yards before the grandstand. Panic reigned for a time as people waited for the gasoline tank to explode. A crowd insisted upon gathering around the blazing car.

After the gasoline tank had been opened, the machine was wheeled off the track. Had the gasoline exploded many believe the track itself would have been consumed. The car is a total loss.

1.—The press stand just after Frank Galvin's car had crashed into it, ... many others. Just behind the overturned car is Dave Lewis, Galvin's team m...
2.—Frank Galvin at the wheel of his Premier, which overturned on the 6...
3.—"Lord" Hughie Hughes, who met death standing at the press stand... Hoskins Special.
4.—Louis Chevrolet, the winner of the event.
5.—The line-up at the start of the race.

Hoskins Done

Continued from First Page.

was entered in both New York and Chicago meets and took fourth and fifth place, respectively. On all occasions that Hughes had driven the Hoskins he has been leading the field only to have tire trouble on each occasion rob him of first place laurels when they were almost in sight.

Johnny Aitken, who with Dario Resta is recognized as one of the best drivers on the track, today in commenting on Hughes, declared:

"Hughie could handle a car that no other man could. He was perhaps one of the most skilled drivers in the game. As an engineer he was perhaps one of the few men who was absolutely acquainted with every part of his machine."

The Oliver First Aid corps, under the direction of Instructor Clyde G. Brehm established a reputation for itself by the quick and adept manner in which care was taken of every injured man on the grounds within two minutes after the accident. Three full teams of the Oliver company were sent to the grounds early in the morning and they were constantly in service. When news of the accident reached the base hospital every man on the grounds was dispatched to the press box. The injured were gathered up quickly and carried to the temporary hospital.

Not only were the first aiders equipped with bandages and a full supply of medical necessities, but the corps also carried a wire cutter with which they were able to break through the safety zone wires and reach the injured. This precaution prevented valuable minutes of delay and possible interruption from the immense crowd who rushed immediately to the spot as word of the accident swept through the grounds.

Everyone of the injured had been taken in hand and was receiving attention at the base hospital within five minutes after the Premier car had made its fatal plunge. Deserved praise was accorded on every side for the methodical, thorough work of the trained first aiders as they carried out the principles of first aid in which they are trained semi-weekly the entire year around.

Physicians who applied bandages and looked after the injured on the grounds were: Dr. C. M. Luman, Dr. A. E. Crow, Dr. J. W. Parshall, Dr. George O. Evans, Dr. Jackson and Dr. Charles W. Utts of Connellsville.

After the injured had been dressed they were taken in the special Oliver first aid hospital truck to the hospital. The Uniontown police patrol augmented this service, Galvin being carried to the hospital in the patrol. The bodies of Hughes and Welsle were hurried to the morgue from the sight of a morbid crowd, many of whom clamored for admission to the hospital to have a look at the dead bodies.

Locked Brakes

Continued from First Page.

press badges were crowded in the flimsy wooden stand when the car swept toward it. Those who saw the tearing four wheeled death dealing contrivance bear down had hardly time to move when a terrific impact, crashing of timber, a swish, and then a heavy thud as the car landed upside down, 100 feet away, gave a fitting impression that something had happened.

The car came diagonally across the track and struck a glancing blow. To this the many in the stand owe their lives. On leaving the wooden surface, the unbridled flyer made another turn which further paralleled the plunging machine with the stand. About 50 of the men in the stand were thrown to the floor and most of those who received injuries were through flying boards.

Hughes, who was to be the car's only victim aside from the occupants, stood several feet from the stand when it tore through. He had just concluded a warm handshake with J. C. Hoskins, owner of the car he drove. Hoskins had congratulated Hughes on his miraculous escape at the northwest turn only five minutes before when to avoid the Pugh Special, Hughes had swung his red speeder, 80 miles an hour, down the track, through the guard rail to possible death for himself and driver.

With the two was M. Worth Colwell, director of publicity. Hughes' exceeded his companion in death.

Galvin first carried a name for himself in the bicycle world. Ten years ago he was recognized as one of the greatest cyclists that ever straddled two wheels. He was the world's greatest pace following rider, and won events with ease in America and Europe. His name was particularly prominent in the Madison Square six day bike events.

WONDERFUL CONSTITUTION

Galvin had an iron frame and a tremendous constitution. He was quiet and likable, courteous to the last degree, and unostentatious at all times in his conduct.

The motor racing game attracted him in 1913 while he toured Europe. His first mount was a German Opel. Winning consistently against heavy odds, Galvin immediately attracted the attention of the owners of famous cars. He started his auto career in American on the Buick "Bug." On the dirt track Galvin was unbeatable.

Then he joined the famous Peugeot team, teaming with Bobby Burman for a while. On one of the western tracks Galvin hit into a collision which sent him to the hospital, where he lingered between life and death for weeks. He carried a silver plate in his skull as a result of the ordeal.

The 1915 season found him back to the track again. This time he took the fast 12-cylinder Sunbeam of Richard Adams. Galvin was in the money at every start. He finished the season with third place at Cincinnati from a field of 12 starters. Early in 1916 he joined the Premier team. At Chicago, in the race which bore him to death Saturday, he finished sixth and at New York in the Harkness trophy race he crossed the line second. In this race he broke all world's records for distance, averaging 106 miles an hour. He finished nine seconds behind his teammate, Johnny Aitken, who won the race.

Galvin lived at New Milford, Connecticut, with his parents until the last few years, when he made his home in New York City. He was 34 years old, and was liked and respected by drivers and track officials alike.

Arrangements for the funeral have not been completed.

Outstanding features today of Saturday's Romantic holiday for which two men delivered their lives on the altar of sport at the Uniontown Speedway were these:

Frank Galvin, driver of the Premier car which made the vicious lunge into the press stand during the 69th lap, died at the Uniontown Hospital at 11:30 Monday morning. His death brings the total up to five.

The official attendance estimated is 12,500. The receipts will total $25,000.

The average speed of Louis Chevrolet, winner of the Universal Film trophy, was 87 miles an hour. Highest speed attained was by Ralph DePalma at 105 miles an hour, in the 76th lap. Repetition of the race on May 12 next will see more drivers of international fame entered. The purse will probably reach $10,000 and among the

Continued on Page Two.

had in their possession.

Both houses passed resolutions to notify the President that they are sitting and ready for his message tomorrow.

The House reconvened at 12:01 when Speaker Clark pounded for order. The Senate got down to business three minutes later. At 12:11 the Senate recessed until 3 o'clock.

Senator Martine, of New Jersey, is another who will fight in the Upper House for a food embargo on all staples. He will introduce a resolution later this week.

Declaring that their work is "dirty, laborious and underpaid," 400,000 of the maintenance departments of American railways today filed a petition with Congress asking to be included in "any eight-hour railroad legislation."

Uniontown Speedway Board Track, 1917

The press stand was rebuilt, and the May 10, 1917, Grand Opening Race at the Uniontown Speedway board track finally arrived. This year, young Billy Taylor from California won the Universal Films Trophy race, his first win, only to lose his life in the war a few months later.

Barney Oldfield had the Golden Submarine built and arrived in Uniontown to show it off, the first race car-with a roof! His friend and rival, Bob Burman, died in a wreck during a race in Corona, California, while rolling his open-cockpit car. After that, Oldfield worked with Los Angeles carburetor developer, Harry Miller, to build a tough, fast car with an enclosed roll cage to protect him. They constructed the Golden Submarine of aluminum. It had holes for the driver to see through. The paint was a mix of bronze dust and lacquer. The historic race-car possessed a four-cylinder aluminum alloy engine, a 104-inch wheelbase, weighed 1,600 pounds and cost $15,000.

The car ran its first race June 1917 on the Chicago Board Speedway. I have photographs of the car here dated May 1917. He did not race it here until 1918. This day he drove a Delage. The master showman shipped the Golden Sub to Uniontown for the big race by way of his own special railroad car. He drove the car in 54 races with 20 wins, but after the engine failed at the 1919 Indianapolis 500, Oldfield retired.

He was so famous by now, that he commanded $4,000 for speaking engagements and $1,000 just to show up at a race. Oldfield was an actor in several films playing a rough and tumble bar room brawler, and remains one of the most well-known names in auto racing history. Because of his promotional skills and extreme driving talents, he parlayed a major career out of the early auto racing and film industries, paving the way for future Speedway Kings.

Barney Oldfield's new Golden Submarine was just unloaded from his private railroad car. August and Fred Duesenberg (two men on the left) look over the car that put their competition, Harry A. Miller and Fred Offenhauser, on the racing map. Charlie Johnson stands behind the car, second from the right.

Barney Oldfield's Golden Submarine #27, Uniontown Train Station, 1917. Charlie Johnson is behind the car to the right. A lefty, he smokes cigar.

Barney Oldfield, standing center, speaks with his protégé, Tommy Milton, before the big grand opening race. Is that Jimmy Murphy in front of the car? The new Press Stand is behind them. Milton had his first win this year for the Duesenbergs on the concrete oval track in Providence, Rhode Island.

The Duesenberg brothers have their hands behind their backs (right). Charlie Johnson is center, sitting sideways in the white hat. These men had never seen a race-car with a roof before. Most had never had the honor of being in the presence of the famous Mr. Oldfield . Here, they surround Oldfield's Golden Submarine as it is unloaded from his railway car at the Uniontown Train Station, May 1917.

Great Throng in Uniontown for the Automobile Races

7,000 PERSONS AT SPEEDWAY BEFORE 11. A. M.

UNIONTOWN SPEEDWAY, May 10.—The crowd began to gather at the track shortly before 11 o'clock this morning, and by noon there were fully 7,000 persons on hand. The West Penn cars were bringing hundreds of people from 10 o'clock on, and there were hundreds of automobiles. Pedestrians were also out in number.

Uniontown is the main bee-hive of the nation today, with all colors, nationalities and ages of humanity swarming here for one of the biggest automobile racing cards ever offered by noted speed demons. Every train and street car arriving in town this morning was crowded to capacity, while a long line of automobiles into the city indicated a monster crowd at the speed saucer this afternoon.

At 11 o'clock there was every indication that Uniontown would have to entertain the largest crowd of its history. In the throng were many notables, including some of the best known automobile men of the world and the star men of many of the big eastern newspapers.

The crowd began arriving late yesterday afternoon, and from that time on there was a steady stream of humanity flowing into the city. By night the strangers had become so great that it was impossible for the hotels and rooming houses to accommodate them, and the result was that large numbers of them slept out, with their suitcases for pillows and their overcoats for bedclothing.

When morning came, each train, each trolley and hundreds of automobiles brought more racing enthusiasts to town. The 9 o'clock Baltimore and Ohio train from West Virginia brought so great a crowd that there was not even standing room in the vestibule. It took a full five minutes for the passengers to leave the train at the Uniontown station. Other trains were almost as crowded, and the specials from Pittsburgh and Fairmont were also filled to capacity.

Today's Racing Program

In the following table, the number of the car as it appears on the course this afternoon, the driver, mechanician and the name of the car is given. The dealers' event is carded for 1 o'clock, Thompson's aeroplane flight for 2:50 and the big race of the day for 3 o'clock.

1 O'CLOCK

DEALERS' RACE—112 MILES.

Car No.	Driver	Mechanician	Car
No. 33—Wilmer Monahan	C. M. Williams	Packar
No. 31—I. P. Fetterman	P. W. Robinson	Peerles
No. 41—Fred McCarthy	R. M. Shoff	Hayne
No. 28—Charles McFarland	Charles Seitz	Murra
No. 32—M. J. Hudoc	D. W. Hickey	Buic
No. 22—H. E. Wynn	L. E. James	Murra
No. 34—H. L. Robinson	E. F. Marsh	Hayne

2:50 O'CLOCK

AEROPLANE FLIGHTS

DeLloyd Thompson, America's Premier Aviator.

3 O'CLOCK

UNIVERSAL TROPHY RACE—112 MILES

Car No.	Driver	Mechanician	Car
No. 1—Louis Chevrolet	Charles Kirkpatrick	Frontenac
No. 14—Ira Vail	Barney Newgard	Hudson
No. 9—Ralph Mulford	Ernest Olsen	Hudson
No. 12—Dave Lewis	Russel Burns	Hoskins
No. 2—Louis Fountaine	H. P. Miller	Mercedes
No. 3—Joe Boyer	Roscoe Searis	Frontena
No. 4—Ralph DePalma	James Steab	Pack
No. 27—Barney Oldfield	Waldo Stein	Oldfield-DeL
No. 42—Andy Burt	M. J. Hudoc	Eri
No. 7—Billy Taylor	M. L. Spence	Newman-Stu
No. 5—Eddie Hearne	Lewis Lecocq	Dusenbe
No. 15—Jimmy Meyer	G. Frazier	Pugl
No. 21—Milt McBride	L. C. Raynor	Olse
No. 24—Art Klein	Wilmer Monahan	Johnson
No. 17—H. E. McCord		Crawford

Gaston Chevrolet in his #44 Frontenac in front of the grandstands.

Tommy Milton in his #7 Duesenberg.

Ralph Mulford prepares for the big race in his #9 Hudson.

It looks like they are pushing Louis Fountain's #2 Mercedes Special. The infield is starting to fill up.

Speedway Kings line up for the Grand Opening race at the Uniontown Speedway. May 10, 1917.

Car #46 takes a spin around downtown Uniontown on its way from the train station to Hopwood.

DeLoyd "Dutch" Thompson, aviator from Washington, Pennsylvania, wows the crowd by dipping and doing somersaults in the sky during intermission.

Billy Taylor wins the Universal Films Trophy, 1917.

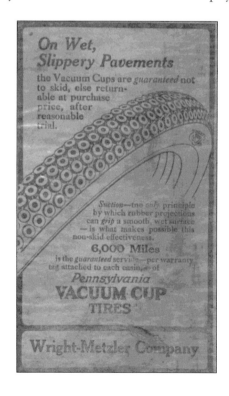

Pete Henderson wrecks his #8 Duesenberg, blowing a tire on "Death's Curve" and hitting the guard rail, unscathed. Autumn Classic, 1917.

Denny Hickey was a local Speedway King who rode as mechanic in the grand opening race but drove Gus Stickel's (Connellsville) #59 Hudson in the Autumn Classic. Hickey went on to place eighth at the Indianapolis 500, winning $1,600. He kept up with the top drivers that day, barely escaping death when he blew a tire. He put on quite a show, spinning in circles, but rolled into the pits waving at the cheering crowd.

Car #54 takes a leisurely spin.

Uniontown Speedway Board Track, 1918

The sun shone over Hopwood for the Liberty Sweepstakes Universal Films Race, May 16, 1918, when the largest crowd yet filled the stands. Throughout the county, roads were jammed. Many people walked to the races, tying their horses off in the woods. A ceremony was held in honor of those who were serving in World War I and 1917 Universal Films Trophy winner Billy Taylor, who was shot down over France.

Veteran racer Barney Oldfield had won several races around the country in his Golden Submarine by now and looked to take the trophy this day.

Louis Chevrolet tails Barney Oldfield's Golden Submarine in a heat to win the World's Track Championship. Oldfield won a pot of gold worth $5,000 in this race. This same year, Harvey Firestone created the Oldfield Tire.

Louis Chevrolet in his #1 Frontenac.

Eddie Hearne driving Chevrolet's Frontenac.

Ralph Mulford's #9 Frontenac before the big race.

L - R (standing): Charlie Johnson, unknown, Dario Resta (won Indy 500 in 1916), Louis Chevrolet (far right). Driver Ralph Mulford wins the third annual Universal Films Trophy. Louis Chevrolet stands in for the deceased Billy Taylor to pass the trophy on to Mulford. May 16, 1918.

In this shot, Universal Films Trophy sponsor Carl "Uncle Carl" Laemmle (right), Universal Films founder and President, poses with trophy. Louis Chevrolet looks on behind Mulford (winner and driver). Dario Resta on left. This is the second year one of Chevrolet's Frontenac race cars took the trophy.

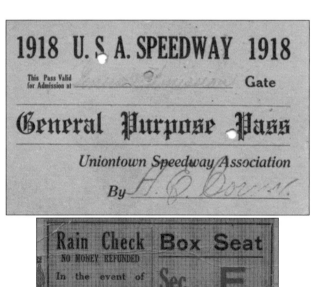

Uniontown Speedway, 1919
#1 Track in America

The May 20, 1919, Universal Films Trophy Race was delayed due to rain. That night, three young prominent Uniontown soldiers went to the crowded Summit Hotel and started a huge brawl with the famous race-car drivers who were partying there.

The next day, in a dead heat between Louis Chevrolet, Tommy Milton, and Ralph Mulford, Milton won the fourth annual Universal Films Trophy Race when Chevrolet's tire exploded from a splinter during the last lap.

The Duesenberg team set 52 AAA records here this year. In the Autumn Classic, three of the four top spots were taken by Frontenacs. Tommy Milton's Duesenberg caught fire, landing him in the Uniontown Hospital for two months.

Place your bets!

The line-up.

Dutch Thompson entertains in his bi plane as Lt. Locklear stands on the upper wing going 60 mph!

Left: Arthur Chevrolet watches the race impatiently when his brother blows a tire that sounds like a high-powered gun shot. Right: Notice the man at the top center of the banked curve. They watched any way they could!

The early July race saw a "scant" crowd of 15,000 due to the rainy forecast. Fifteen hundred soldiers watched Milton win both the first and final heats. These are photographs of the Victory Parade held that day in downtown Uniontown.

The Fayette County Court House during the WWI Victory Parade.

L – R: Uniontown Country Club; Uniontown High School.

L-R: Neil Whalen, Uniontown Speedway Manager of Events and Flagman, Whalen's wife and silent film star Vivian Prescott, and Tommy Milton. Milton tried hard to hide the fact that he was blind in one eye and was known as a flirt. Right photo: Even the sponsors need a push at times.

GIRL TO COMPETE IN LONG AUTOMOBILE RACE.

PHILADELPHIA, April 8.—The only permission ever granted to a woman auto driver to compete in the races at Indianapolis has been won by Miss Vivian Prescott of 904 North Broad street, this city, the daring young driver who created a sensation at the Vanderbilt Cup races by taking part in the death-dealing course disguised as a mechanician and riding with Neil Whalen, the National driver.

In the Autumn Classic, Tommy Milton hit a hole in the wooden track on Death Curve, breaking a connecting rod. The dead cylinder filled with gas. When the Duesenberg back-fired, it caught on fire. Milton spent two months in the Uniontown Hospital. His mechanic, W.D. Kessler, fell in love with their nurse, Gladys Bean, married her, and moved to Uniontown. Milton took his own life in 1962, due to the pain he still suffered from these severe burns.

Joe Boyer replaced Gaston Chevrolet in the Frontenac when Chevrolet came into the pits to reshod. Boyer took the big race this day, September 3, 1919.

Uniontown Speedway Board Track, 1920

In 1920 the Volstead Act outlawed spirits with more than 5 percent alcohol. Prohibition began. Regardless, the largest crowd ever (50,000!) enjoyed a gorgeous summer day this June 21 at the greatest race track in America.

Tommy Milton won the Universal Films Trophy again, followed by his Duesenberg team. Second, Third and Fourth places were taken by Jimmy Murphy, Eddie O'Donnell, and I.P. "Red" Fetterman of Pittsburgh. This is the last year Milton drove for the Duesenbergs.

Although the track entertained the wealthiest in the nation, at this point, it was deteriorating. Large splinters filled radiators. Big holes needed fixed, and Uniontown Speedway President Charlie Johnson promised to have the repairs completed by the next year's race.

Jimmy Murphy, left, looking at the camera, and Ralph Mulford, standing, await the start of the race.

Denny Hickey in Gus Stickel's #59 Hudson.

Ansterberg's Frontenac.

L – R: Roscoe Searle's Monroe Frontenac. Red Fetterman's #49 Peerless.

Gaston Chevrolet in his new Frontenac. Brother Louis built this car for Gaston. He was killed in it later that year in Beverly Hills. Louis never raced again after Gaston's fatal accident. There is a man with a bicycle in back of the car. I do not see a motor on it.

Frontenac lineup: Roscoe Searles #8, Gaston Chevrolet #1, and Ernie Ansterberg's #5.

Left: Car #53.   Right: The Duesenberg brothers check out a car I have yet to identify. The driver looks like Jimmy Murphy to me.

The top left note says, "Freddie Frame, a first class mechanic in the shop. When at home could operate any machine in the shop. Did some riding as mechanic. Rarely drove for Tommy Milton at races." Notice the B & D on the boards to the right under the new air compressor. This is part of a Black & Decker/Duesenberg promotion.

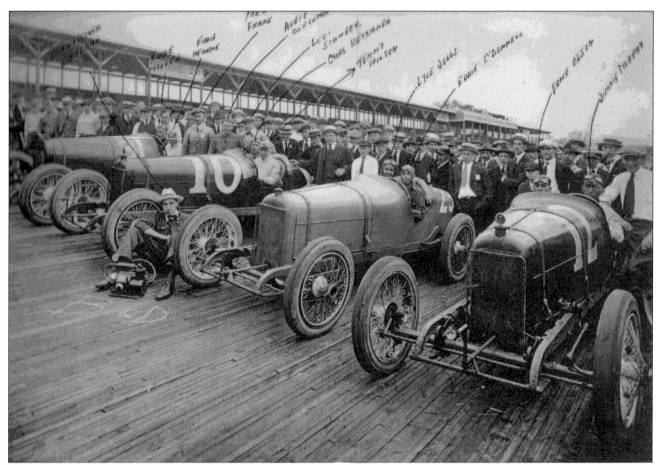

This is a beautiful shot of Duesenbergs. I believe this is from an advertising promotion for the new Black and Decker compressor. In addition to the above-named, Charlie Johnson is standing to the right of Milton's Duesenberg #10 and has his hand on the back of it. He is wearing a white hat. Vivian Prescott's face is peeking through directly behind Eddie O'Donnell. She is in a dark hat looking over her son's shoulder. Fred Duesenberg is to the left, just behind his brother, Augie, who is to the left of Milton's car. It looks like the Black & Decker Salesman (seated) has the new compressor at his feet. Notice that Murphy's Duesie on the right shows the dropped axle and offset spindle the Duesie team invented that year.

Uniontown Speedway Board Track, 1921

More than 50,000 spectators filled the Uniontown Speedway June 18, 1921, with expectations of seeing Milton retain the title. If he won a third time, he could keep the trophy. The sixth annual Universal Films Trophy Race was the biggest event of the year in America's racing game.

Searles won the big race in his Duesie #6, which was Milton's #10 from the year before. In addition to the trophy, he won $5,000. Milton took 8th place in a new Frontenac.

Uniontown and the mountains were filled with revelers. Parties at the Titlow and Summit Hotels went on into the night. George Titlow reported serving 900 loaves of bread and thousands of dinners. I wonder how much rye was served on the 4th floor, reserved for barons and celebrities.

The curves of the Uniontown Speedway board track were banked at 34 degrees, allowing speed records to be set that were impossible to achieve at Indianapolis. The banner to the right has a hand pointing to the left and says "Tunnel to Grand Stand."

The 1921 line up…

Chevrolet's Frontenacs lineup.

Pittsburgh's I. P. "Red" Fettermen, left, became a real contender here. He poses on his Peerless.

Tommy Milton's Frontenac chassis with new Duesenberg block.

Roscoe Searles' Duesie takes Death's Curve to win the 6th annual Universal Films Trophy Race.

Uniontown Speedway Board Track, 1922

Before the 7th annual Universal Films Race, drivers promoted the big event on the radio for the first time. Pittsburgh's KDKA interviewed Barney Oldfield, Jimmy Murphy, Tommy Milton, Red Fetterman, and Harry Harris.

It is said that through the years, the box office of the Uniontown Speedway was run in a very loose manner. Oftentimes investors would walk in and take a fistful of cash from the wooden barrels where it was kept. It is also reported that the money was left unattended quite often. The Uniontown Speedway Association filed for bankruptcy, and Mrs. Brownfield, owner of the property, requested an injunction against them. The race did go on, but the track was still in need of extensive repair.

Ticket sales were brisk, and Jimmy Murphy won the race in his #12 Duesenberg. This is the same car he won the Indy 500 and French Grand Prix in that year. The car is displayed in the Indy Museum. Murphy was the first American to win the French Grand Prix.

After this race, Charlie Johnson, Uniontown Speedway Association President, took the proceeds and went to Cuba for 18 years. This action closed the famous track, soiled the town's national reputation, and sent Uniontown into an economic downward spiral.

The track was torn apart by area residents through the years. Many local buildings, porches, and chicken coops were built from its lumber.

Of the 24 big races and heats (that I am aware of) held at the Uniontown Speedway board track, 6 were won my Tommy Milton, 3 by Louis Chevrolet, 3 by Ralph Mulford, 2 by Eddie Hearne, 2 by Roscoe Searles (had been Chevrolet's mechanic), 2 by I.P. Fetterman, and 1 each by Billy Taylor, Frank Elliot, Dave Lewis, Barney Oldfield, Gaston Chevrolet/Joe Boyer, and Jimmy Murphy. Boyer, Searles, Chevrolet, Mulford, Chevrolet's Frontenacs, Duesenbergs, and Miller cars won these races. Details can be found in my earlier book, *Yesteryear at the Uniontown Speedway*.

1922 lineup.

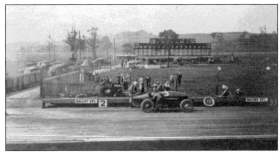
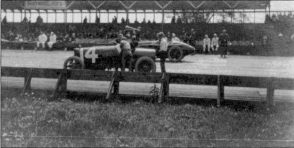

Ralph Mulford's Frontenac #10.

Louis Chevrolet on left with mechanic.

Henry Chevrolet.

 Pushing the motorcycle in for repairs.

This is the only photograph I have found of a motorcycle racing on the Uniontown Board Track.

Bikes line up. I do not see a motor on the closest bike.

Jimmy Murphy's #12 Miller – Duesenburg won the 7th Annual Universal Films Trophy Race, June 17, 1922. Jimmy Murphy is the last man to win the Universal Films Trophy. He died in a wreck in 1924.

Jimmy Murphy set the high speed record here at 109.46 mph.

Before each race at the Uniontown Speedway Board track, a panoramic photograph was taken of the drivers, mechanics, and sponsors. Many of them are published in my book, *Yesteryear at the Uniontown Speedway*.

The June 17, 1922, photograph is particularly important. This was the last race held here because the track was deteriorating. I have many photographs of Charlie Johnson in both Speedway books. He is in a three-piece suit and hat in every photo but this one. It seems he is dressed to travel in his casual wear and sunglasses. Note that in the more than 200 photos I have of this track, this is the only instance where someone is wearing shades. It is my belief that he is covering his eyes this day so he does not give away his intentions through them. The former Speed King looks a bit thin and sad here, as he plans to rob many of the wealthiest men in the country, disappoint thousands of race fans, and shame Uniontown.

Through the years, George Titlow, promoted Fayette County in addition to his own interests He sold his internationally popular hotel in 1922, saying, "You can't run a hotel without spirits." Johnson had spent a lot of time at the Titlow Hotel, which sat less than a block from his Standard Garage. He met Titlow's wealthy, famous friends there and had been accepted into their world.

Johnson returned to Uniontown and even spoke at the Bryson Uniontown Speedway dedication in 1940. George Titlow died in his lawyer's office two days later. You be the judge of what caused his heart attack. He had just told Judge Henderson that he never felt better. He made his daughter wait downstairs, although he was elderly and used a cane.

The only person I have met who ever spoke with Charlie Johnson is Jim Campbell, 96, of Uniontown. He relayed two downtown encounters to me as follows. In the late 1930's - It could have been 1940, Campbell witnessed Johnson hitting a young man's car with his. Johnson was yelling at the teenager and in the process of taking him around the corner to "convince" him that Johnson himself was in the right. Campbell walked over and flashed a deputy badge he used doing investigative research. He told Johnson he could write him up a ticket then and there. Johnson jumped into his car and took off, much to the teen's relief. Campbell referred to Johnson as a "rascal."

Another day, Campbell and Johnson ran into each other on West Main Street. Johnson pointed out the building at Peter and Arch Streets where his Standard Garage had been for many years. He told Campbell that he had built three race cars there. He also sold Packard automobiles.

I have scanned the very wide panoramic picture in sections. They are here in order, from left to right, as in the shot taken that historical day.

This is the far left part of the panoramic photo. No one knew it was the final race but Uniontown Speedway Association President Charlie Johnson. Look closely at the boards. Rough riding! There were huge holes in the track and had been for several years. It was a job for Neil Whalen to keep drivers away from them. Boys also hid under the track, popping their heads up through the holes, ducking when the cars got close! I have yet to find a photo of that. Stay tuned.

Above Left to Right: Unknown, Dwight Kessler (Duesenberg mechanic), George Stiehl (Tommy Milton's mechanic), Herschel McKee (Elliot's mechanic), Harlan Fengler (Hartz mechanic), Tommy Milton.

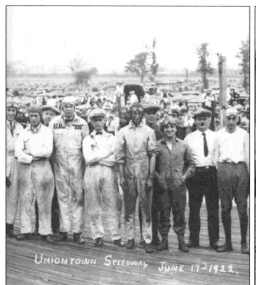

Left to Right: Harry Hartz, Ernie Olsen, Gus Stickel (Connellsville Car Owner), Frank Elliot, unknown, unknown, Jimmy Henderson, Marcel Tregoox, Arthur Chevrolet, Steve Nemesh, (twice), Glen Howard, Unknown, Leon Dower, Louis Chevrolet, unknown, Fred Duesenberg, Ralph Mulford, Ira Vail, August Duesenberg, Ora Haibe.

Augie Duesenberg, Ora Haibe, Shorty Hansen, Dario Resta, Jack Curtner, unknown, Tom Rooney, next seven unknown, Thane Houser (in white coveralls), unknown, unknown, I.P. "Red" Fetterman.

Left to Right: I.P. Fetterman, Ora Raibe, unknown, unknown, Neil Whalen, Manager of Events, Charlie Johnson (in sunglasses), Whalen's son (twice), next four unknown, Barney Oldfield with goggles on head.

Jimmy Murphy (right) just before winning the last Universal Film Trophy Race, 1922.

After the Board Track

During the writing of this book, I heard from many interesting characters. I was particularly thrilled when a former Connellsville resident contacted me. His father, race car driver, Lou Falcone, drove during the Jennerstown Speedway's early years. He was a friend of Denny Hickey. The family believes it was Hickey who encouraged Falcone to drive.

Left: Hudson factory built Indianapolis racecar. It appears to be the car driven by Denny Hickey in 1919. Hickey is standing front right. Right: Lou Falcon in his Frontenac SR4 posed in Dunbar, Pennsylvania. The site is across Bridge Street where Lou operated an auto repair garage and gas Station. The shop building also served as fire truck garage/storage for the Dunbar Volunteer Fire Department.

The following letter tells the tale:

Owner-driver, Lou Falcone, was born in Connellsville, Pennsylvania on December 29, 1902. When the family relocated to Los Angeles in 1942, he changed his last name into "Falcon." Louie's father, John, was a cement contractor in Connellsville and provided the paving for many of the town's sidewalks. As the practice was in those days, an imprint with the contractor's name was placed at each end of the pavement strip.

  In 1915, Lou dropped out of school. He was in the seventh grade, and found work at an automobile repair shop. It is our estimation that former race car driver, Denny Hickey, inspired Lou to become involved in local auto racing. The car he crafted was a type known as a "Three Quarters" car that dimensionally was ¾ the size of the "Big Cars" that raced at Indianapolis and the many board tracks around the U.S. The three-quarter-type car was raced on tracks of one-half mile, usually with a dirt surface. Many of these tracks were county fairground horse tracks. Present day cars of this sort are known as Sprint Cars.

  As a rule most racecars are classed by wheelbase, the measurement between the front and wheel centers with the wheels set straight ahead. In the day, the Big Cars were limited to a minimum 100 inch wheelbase and the Three Quarter cars minimum was 75 inches, much shorter and better for the smaller tracks. The engine sizes were also controlled on the same basis. The majority of the Three-Quarter cars were home-built, utilizing parts from passenger cars. On a national basis there was a big supply network of special racing parts available by mail order, just like today.

We do not know when Lou and friends built the first car but assume that it was in the early to mid 1920s. This car was a much modified Model T Ford. The frame had been narrowed to a width just wide enough for a single person. To accomplish this task a standard Ford frame, standing alone, had the cross members removed and replaced by shorter units. These were welded, bolted or riveted into place. The standard Ford front and rear suspension and steering was installed. Racing friction disk shock absorbers were also added. The Model T Ford engine was modified with the addition of a Frontenac overhead valve cylinder head (aka. "Fronty" manufactured by the Chevrolet brothers at Indianapolis, Indiana) and a racing carburetor. Other internal parts were replaced with racing units and a dual externally driven magneto ignition system replaced the Ford unit that was internal with the flywheel. The standard Ford transmission and clutch system was retained. Special quick change, center lock, 30 by 3 -½ inch tires and wire wheels were added. The body, crafted along racecar lines with a cowl and tail, were fabricated using pieces of standard auto bodywork that offered the compound curves.

This car was raced at every available event in venues located in southwestern Pennsylvania, West Virginia and Maryland. Lou was particularly fond of racing at Jennerstown, PA, because he could park the family car on a hill that overlooked one turn of the oval track. The turn was carved out of the terrain that resulted in a very steep embankment. He would remove the seats out of the family car so we could all sit on them to watch the race, which were usually 100-mile events.

Lou burst into the lead passing three cars in one turn to take the lead in the 1930 Jennerstown Speedway Labor Day race. The car hooked a rut in the track surface, abruptly turned right and struck the above mentioned embankment, went straight up-nose high and came to rest on the racetrack tail first. Lou was partially out of the cockpit. The headrest struck his back fracturing a vertebra. The resulting shock propelled his 135-pound body out of the car and onto the track in front of the oncoming herd of cars. One of Lou's crew, Tony Fiesta, was in the infield on the turn. He sprinted onto the track and dragged Lou to the safety of the infield. He "sprinted" very fast for a man with a prosthetic leg in 1930.

I was a mere 2 years, 3 months old when this accident happened and I remember viewing it. My mother, who was not a fan of racing, claims that I was hit with pieces that flew off the car but she tended to be overly theatrical about this sort of thing. I do recall that he was bedridden at home a long time recovering from his broken back.

Another memory was that my very first rides in a racecar on a racetrack were on his lap during warm-ups. The organizers permitted this practice as long as the speeds were slow. Dad had a small helmet and goggles made for me to wear when riding with him. Many of my present day friends ask how long I have been in auto racing and my response is, "Nearly 81 years…." I reckon that qualifies me as a real "Old-timer."

After the crash, Lou and the crew built another car using what was salvageable from "The SR-4 Fronty." It is understood that there was a rule change that handicapped the "Fronty's" so a Rajo head was used on the new car. Lou drove it for a while then, due to home pressure, stepped out of the cockpit and made it available for younger guys who had the desire. My thought is that he sold it around 1934 or 35 when he purchased a new family car, a 1934 Huppmobile Aero Sedan that was styled by Raymond Lowey. The styling was very aerodynamic for the era and much better looking than the Chrysler AirFlow models. Our family made three Pennsylvania to Los Angeles round trips in that car. It was so rare that it turned heads in each small town we drove through, cruising US Routes 40 and 66 on our transcontinental voyages.

One of the interesting things about Lou's life is that he remained active in auto racing long after he retired as an active participant. The final family move to Southern California was prompted by the outbreak of WW II and the large number of aircraft companies located there. Lou was too old at that time to gain employment at one of the factories. The Personnel guy at AiResearch Manufacturing pointed out that he could do his part for the War Effort by keeping the aircraft workers cars operational…public transportation being what it was in the area at that time.

He leased a large vacant gasoline station in Culver City and eventually moved his auto wheel alignment equipment from Connellsville to Culver City and into the repair shop area. He rented out the gas station and the remaining service bays. At the time, Culver City was home to three major motion picture studios and at the end of WW II it became a racecar fabrication and equipment mecca. By that time he had built a new building that was home to four auto wheel alignment stations along with wheel balancing and straightening. One alignment station was dedicated to frame straightening. The shop soon became a place where all sorts of racecars and interesting motor vehicles appeared for Lou Falcon Wheel Alignment's specialized service.

Lou became acquainted with a fellow auto repairman who owned an auto brake specialty shop and was interested in racing sports cars. Calculating that Lou's racing experience would be very helpful with setting up his racing program, Lou gladly helped Joe Playan with his series of cars that began with a Jaguar XK20 Coupe to an MG Special to a Porsche 550 Spyder. Serving as Joe's mechanic, he became the first American to completely disassemble the very complex Porsche 550, flat four cylinder engine, with bevel gear driven dual overhead camshafts. He accomplished this overhaul and re-assembly without benefit of a technical manual for reference. There were no existing manuals at the time except for those at the dealerships, and they were reluctant to share any knowledge because they wanted the repair work for their service department. When the crowd assembled in Joe's shop to see if the engine would ever run again, at the first exhaust bark, money changed hands!

Lou crossed Life's Finish Line on July 10, 1989 due to heart failure. He was 86 years old. Prior to his death, as he laid in a coma in the hospital, I made certain that his room TV was tuned to the Indy 500 and the volume was turned up high. Coma or not, I know he heard the broadcast.

Lou inspired this writer, his son, who became an active participant and contributor to all forms of auto racing and has maintained this prominence for nearly 60 years. Thanks to Lou our family has been involved in auto racing for over 100 years now and there is another generation ready to follow in his footsteps.

Bob Falcon

 Lil Bobby posed in Daddy's Fronty-Prior to 1930

Photos L – R: Lou's New Rajo Ford that replaced the crashed Fronty. This photo was taken in front of Lou's relocated shop that was on Ninth Street in Connellsville. The driver is unknown. Right: The Rajo and the crew in front of the Connellsville shop. Left to Right; Unk, Unk, Jeff, Tony Fiesta seated in car, Unk and Tony's brother Sully.

Photos L – R: John Fiesta and Bob Falcon in 1940. The two were neighborhood grammar school chums. Center: Lou works on Playan's MG Special at Torry Pines, 1950's. Right: Lou sheds a tear over the remains of son Bob's 32 Ford coupe after a 200-foot "endo" tumble down the front straight at Long Beach Stadium. (1955)

More Local Board Tracks

The Altoona Speedway board track (above) ran from 1923 – 1931.

Bridgeville, PA had a ½ mile board track for a short period.

There were 24 board tracks, they say, but most only ran two to three years. The Uniontown Speedway was the most famous due to its long run and the extraordinarily rich famous men who backed it. During its rein, it was one of only a few tracks. Most ran before or after the 1916 – 1922 time period. Board tracks often closed due to deaths from extraordinary speed, and the cost of maintaining the tracks was high. WW I and the depression were also issues.

The Jennerstown Speedway was built during the Altoona track's demise. This ran from 1928/9 to 2008, a remarkable run as far as race tracks go. It went from being a flat ½ mile dirt track to a ¼ mile dirt oval in 1953.

By then Heidelberg was in full swing (1948 – 1973). A ½ mile oval was reconstructed in the 1960's at Jennerstown, but this was a short run. In 1967 Piney Laskey and associates purchased the track. They raced sprint cars for a great twenty seasons. Laskey took the ball after that, turning it into an asphalt track. He put money into the grandstands and concessions, and hooked up with NASCAR before dying in 1994. The track has changed hands several times since, before closing. You will see photographs through the years in this book from Jennerstown and Heidelberg…and some tracks we can not yet identify!

In 1940, the Bryson brothers of Uniontown built a dirt track inside the old Uniontown Speedway board track. It had asphalt curves. As stated earlier, Charlie Johnson, who ran off with the board track proceeds eighteen years before, spoke at the dedication of this track. This is a shot from a 1947 race held there. Hopwood, PA.

I mentioned that I have photos from unknown local tracks. The following photographs are circa 1950 somewhere in the region. There were so many dirt tracks. Any ideas?

I love the wagon wheel bumper.

I believe the Krafick coupe is from Vandergrift's Krafick Auto Wreckers.

Guseman's Uniontown Speedway

In the early 1950's, William Guseman of Uniontown, built a state-of-the-art race track where the Kennedy School was later constructed. His son, Donald, lost his life here in 1953. Many locals loved this track and have very fond memories of G.T. George, Pappy Cornish, Mel Minnick, Sr., Buts Buterbaugh and Banty Workman, racing their coupes. Jack Ruckus drove for Cornish. His wife said that he raced so much, the only time he saw his daughter was at the races!
And here is the line-up…

Leonard Richezza, #35 Jr., is racing by. The sign says, "AAA Midget Auto races, Aug. 28."

Earl "Banty" Workman is upside down in his "Beast" on the guard rail. His daughter remembers him getting hurt this day.

Powder puff races were also held here occasionally. A local girl named Ruby McMahon tells me that she raced here twice, winning $10. each time for coming in second behind Carolyn Boyd…until her father made her stop!

Standing: Sam Shaffer and Bill "Buts" Buterbaugh. Kneeling: Jim Stone. Buts' car #95.

But's wife, Loretta, said that while Buts was racing at Morgantown one evening, they announced to him and the crowd that she had just given birth to twins. "He kept driving!" she laughed.

Paul Smith works on G.T. George's #145 Hudson Hornet. Garry Sisson, G.T.'s cousin, said of George, "He was a front end specialist ahead of his time, with technical insight."

Paul Smith in G.T. George's #145. L.J. Dennis said that he saw Bob Arsenberger wreck way back when at Morgantown. "It was the worst I ever saw. The car came apart!" I asked Bob about the crash. He said, "G.T. called to see if I would drive his Hornet because Bill Dull said it wasn't safe. I was 19. Mel Minnick, spun out in front of me. I went up over Mel, end over end. We only had a lap seat belt. I lost my shoes and wallet. Got beat up." This was 1963, going 50 – 60mph. He kept racing!

More Local 1940's - 1950's photos…

Banty Workman, of Grindstone, PA, with his #35 "Beast," late 1940's.

Banty Workman leans on the front of the truck. His "Beast" is in front of Bob Shaw's Garage which was located on Hopwood Coolspring Road. Clyde Shaw and Bob Shaw, Jr. are beside #35. Bob Shaw, Sr. is behind the car. 1953/54

In 1952, Elkins, W.V. saw the opening of a popular dirt track. In 1956, the Morgantown Speedway opened. Many of the men who raced at Guseman's and Jennerstown, also raced at these much-loved and missed tracks, in addition to Heidelberg, which opened in 1948. The Thornton track in Brownsville was a ¼ mile dirt track in two locations from 1951-53, run by Lester Cutty Mairs.

Elkins Raceway, 1952. This was their first race!

Jim and Rena Cryster's Morgantown Speedway ran from 1956 through 1978. This is Jim with "Ole Lil." He was a mechanic in the coal mines. "He hauled pipe railing from the mines and built the rails and bleachers at the track. The fence, too!" Bud Cryster said. "Dad got barred from other tracks, so he bought into one," Bud laughed"

Howard Bramner owned this car. It was driven by Gary McCullough.
Sept. 7, 1957, Morgantown Speedway.

Rick and Jeff Henry pose with Dirt Henry's first race car, 1959. Dirt said that he only drove once, at Guseman's. Buts Buterbaugh informed him that he was not welcome there. He never drove again, but has backed his sons and others ever since. Dirt is 85 years old at this writing.

I love this shot of Dick Linder's Sportsman Coupe V-2, owned by the Palone Brothers in Rice's Landing. Linder raced often at Heidelberg and area tracks, competing with local greats like Herb Scott, Buddy O'Connor, and Lou Blaney. Linder died in an accident in New Jersey in 1959 at age 35, only a month before his chance to qualify for the Indy 500. Here, he obviously just replaced the V-2's body (was bright yellow). Early 1950's.

Heidelberg Raceway

Speedway Kings of the 1960's

This section of the book is dedicated to the many Speedway Kings I interviewed for this book, their comrades, crews, and all local Speedway Kings and pit crews in the region, now and yesteryear. This book is a representation of the consistent hard work and focus a man can have when he knows he will get to go very fast very soon, with a shot at the checkered flag.

The last question of each interview was always the same, "Why do you do it?"

The answers, you will see, were a little different, but similar.

Pam Bendishaw said it best when I asked her about Jimmy, Sr. "He had a need for speed," she said, shaking her head affirmatively. I agreed, and that sums it up for many men and women. Like these…

Left: Bob Arsenberger, late 1960's. Right: Henry Motor Sales, early 1960's

In 1966, L.J. Dennis hit the dirt track racing scene with his Rainbow #7.

When asked why the car was painted this way, L.J. said that his brother used up all the remains in the many paint cans sitting around the garage to create this bit of racing history.

Left: Banty Workman with Bounce Hager's Fun Seeker, 1964. Right: Russ Redshaw's wrecked Chevelle. He rebuilt this car with his wife's Chevelle, without her knowledge. She forgave him later, when she was driving a newer model. This is a racer's wife's life!

Left: Dirt Henry bought this car from Jim Reid in Daytona for $1500. in 1964. That car worked out so well, they bought the car on the right from Reid in 1969 for Gary Henry to drive.

Left: Buts Buterbaugh takes the checkered flag at Elkins, 1965. Right: Bill Frehaufer driving Johnny Orbin's car at the Schmuckers Speedway in Latrobe, 1965.

Garry Sisson, age 17, receives his first checkered flag, 1969. Frank Baker, right, was the much-beloved Morgantown Speedway Flagman. "Frank could get out of the way of the cars quick. He had no stand! He and his wife, Jean, were instrumental in the success of the track," Bud Cryster said.

"My dad took me to Morgantown Speedway, and G.T. George, took me everywhere back in the day, Jennerstown Speedway, the old Latrobe Speedway. It was against the rules to have kids in the pits but he'd sneak me in. I used to sit on the tow truck's roof, wrapped around the bubble light. Once I was hurrying to get something to eat and a tire came flying and hit me. It scared us to death, and G.T. quit taking me with him for a while, but eventually he gave in," Garry smiled. "As kids we would buy old cars for fifty dollars and race them in the old Guseman's Speedway field."

Left: Fred Johnson in his sprint car #56, 1965. Right: Johnson improves on the wings for traction, 1966, Morgantown Speedway. Johnson's garage was very near the track, at the Cheat exit.

feature contest on the program for semi-late model cars.

Other Winners

The first of the four ten lap tests was won by Sam Meyers, of Baltimore. Turk Burkett, Claysburg, was second and Ed Deiwiler, Mt. Pleasant, Pa., third.

Other leaders were:

Second Race—1. Ray Fanning, Baltimore. 2. Bood Lodge, Bridgeport, W. Va. 3. Dencil Dillman, Hyland, Md.

Third Race—1. Clayton Housted, Philipsburg, Pa. 2. Jim Nare, Bedford, Pa. 3. Charles Werman, Dallastown, Pa.

Fourth Race—1. L. J. Dennis, Markleysburg, Pa. 2. Bill Rausch, Bethel Park, Pa. 3. Bob Boyle, Parkersburg, W. Va. 4. John Meeker, Glen Burnie, Md.

Consolation: 1. Ron Dolen, Zanesville, Ohio. 2. Carl Smith, Mt. Pleasant, Pa. 3. Bus Brossemeire, Ellicott City, Pa.

Most of the dropouts in the main event attributed their trouble to broken front end frames.

Turk Burkett, popular driver, of Claysburg, Pa., entered two cars in the races but one was disqualified because it was without a transmission and was illegal. Some of his followers demanded their money back and they received it — then saw the races from grandstand seats.

David L. Molinari, 29, of New Carrollton, Md., one of the drivers, suffered lacerations of the face near the left eye and was treated at a local hospital and released.

Bob McGinley, Georgetown, Pa., was the official announcer and Robert "Smokey" Epley, president of the National Association of Starters and Flagmen, was the starter.

Plan Program Oct. 22

John Barton, racing director, announced that plans are under way to stage races for supermodifieds at Cumberland Raceway on Sunday, October 22.

Left: Jean Baker wrote the track stats for the local newspaper. Right: L.J. Dennis won 151 features in his career. There was even a bounty on his head!

Lawrence Dennis Win

Markleysburg Driver Earns $1,000 Purse

Cops $100 For Best Qualifying Time; 4,100 See Races

A consistent winner on West Virginia quarter-mile ovals, Lawrence J. Dennis, 33, son of a Markleysburg, Pa., lumber dealer, made his debut at the Cumberland Raceway Sunday and became the first winner of the East Coast 100 before approximately 4,100 spectators.

Dennis, who won his 50th feature race Friday at Elkins, outlasted a field of 33 starters, 12 of whom finished, over the local half mile oval and collected top prize of $1,000, the biggest purse he has received in two years of racing.

Tom Colella, of Whitehall, Pa., finished second in the feature event and earned $600 while Ed Duvall, Baltimore, who came in third, received $400. Fourth place, worth $300, went to Alton Duley, Morgantown, W. Va. Gene Saine, Baltimore, was fifth and he was the recipient of $200.

Dennis received an additional $100 for turning in the fastest qualifying time on the preliminary card of five ten-lap contests.

A total of $4,500 was distributed among the drivers in the feature contest on the program

Speedway Kings, 1970's

The Heidelberg Speedway closed in 1973 and Morgantown's last race was run in 1978. The Latrobe Speedway opened in 1977 and Pittsburgh's Pennsylvania Speedway, in 1979. There were and are, more tracks, Ruffsdale, Motordrome 70 Speedway, St. Clairsville, etc. These are a collection of photos, not a complete history…of a whole lot of racing going on.

Bud Cryster, Jr. in the Morgantown Speedway pace car, 1970's.

While interviewing men who raced, worked, and played at the Morgantown Speedway, I spoke with Lou Ansel. He began towing cars there with his father and Speedy Sterbutzel at age 13. Although he cried because of the noise there when he was 4 years old, by now he loved the sound, smells, and excitement the race track offered. He also liked the hot dogs the men made in the pits, "They were the best!" he smiled, remembering…women were not allowed int the pits back then."

Left: Bernard Keene Right: Jack Smith, 1970's

Bob Arsenberger gets the checkered flag at Morgantown Speedway, early 1970's. His wife, daughter, and mother join in the celebration.

Larry Baker takes the checkered flag in his 1957 Chevy at the Morgantown Speedway, 1975.

Mel Minnick, Sr., Morgantown Speedway, early 1970's.

Dom "Neener" Masi, Morgantown Speedway, early 1970's.

Russ Redshaw wins at Jennerstown, 1977.

BIG WEEKEND — Two of the district's top race drivers, Dom Masi of Uniontown, left, and Russ Redshaw of West Leisenring, right, face a heavy card this weekend. Masi will enter his 1957 Chevy and Redshaw will be behind the wheel of his 1964 Chevelle at North Hills tonight, Lernerville Friday, Morgantown Saturday, the Motordrome on Sunday and North Hills again on Monday. Both cars are classed in the semi-late division. Masi, who has already won two titles at Lernerville and another at Morgantown, won the 1971 championship at Lernerville. Redshaw, the 1971 king at the Motordrome, has won at Lernerville once this year.

Russ Redshaw (62), L.J. Dennis (7), and Blackie Watt battle it out at Motordrome 70 Speedway, 1976.

Left: Tom Baxter, right, working on L.J. Dennis' Rainbow 7. Dennis leans on the car in blue, 1973.
Right: Dennis rounds the bend in early 1970's at the Motordrome Spedway.

If I learned nothing during the writing of this book, I do now know that a driver can not function without a top notch, dedicated crew. L. J. Dennis thanks his…

Wayne Hager , Ron Bryner, L. J. Dennis, Tom Baxter - The Rainbow 7 Crew, 1970's

Butterbaugh Race Winner

That was some kind of race Saturday night as Uniontown's Richard Butterbaugh withstood all challenges to finish first in the 30 lap cadet feature at Morgantown Speedway.

A total of 24 cadet cars out of 37 qualified for the cadet race with Butterbaugh trailing Garry Sisson of Uniontown for the first seven laps.

Because of restarts and pile-ups only nine cars finished the race. Butterbaugh fought off Bernard Keene during the last five laps to get the win.

Butterbaugh also won the first heat in the cadet division, two Uniontown drivers placed in the second heat with Russ Redshaw winning and Dom Masi placing third. Sisson got a 10th place in the feature.

In the late model competition, Markleysburg's L. J. Dennis placed second in the helmet dash behind Steve Helmick.

L.J.Dennis, center with trophy, Bobby Lake, far right – Morgantown Speedway 1970's. Dennis won over 150 features in his long standing career. He even drove a time or two at Roaring Knob this season, 2011. Jack Smith (car owner) to left of L.J.

Bobby Lake has been involved in racing for 35 years. "L.J. and the crew showed up on my 16th birthday, and again on my 50th," he smiled.
When I asked L. J. why he did it, spent so much time, effort, and ingenuity racing, he jumped out of his chair, clenched his fists at his side and almost yelled, "I gotta win!"

And win, he has.

I have seen many a transport, but loved this shot of L.J. Dennis' bus. They are loading the Rainbow 7, 1970's.

Russ Redshaw thanks his crew. Standing: Redshaw, Butch Grubbs. Kneeling: John Redshaw, Ron Grubbs. Photo taken at car show, Uniontown Mall, Spring 1977.

Dick Rugh's second drag car, Pittsburgh, 1970's.

Dick Rugh credits his brother, Jake, with guiding him from the time he was 6 years old, to the right tools for the right job.

Dick Rugh's older brother, Jake, had cerebral palsy. He had no use of his hands, had one good foot, was intelligent, but could not communicate with most people. As kids, Dick and his brother, Alf, helped their father make Jake a walker with bicycle wheels on casters so that Jake could go play in the fields, too. Throughout their lives, Jake had a tool room. He kept it organized and clean.

In the above 1946 photograph, the Rugh siblings ride their wagon to Smithfield, selling apples door to door. Dick was 10 years old. Jake was 18. Three years later, the boys rebuilt an old Model A Ford, cutting off its roof with a hatchet. They would put Jake in the driver's seat of the convertible so he could use his good foot while they steered through the fields.

From 1959 – 1967, Dick worked at Fayette Parts where he met G.T. George, Art Cornish, and Banty Workman. "G.T. is the most intelligent man I have ever dealt with. He was 20 years ahead of his time, quiet, brilliant. A smart cookie."

In 1961, Dick heard a sound that drew him in and never let him go. He was at Fort Bragg, and they were go karts. That's when the racing bug began for Rugh. He opened an independent auto parts store in 1968 and has evolved to build racing motors. By 1970 he already built a drag car for Fred Close. He has been building drag and stock ever since.

"I dream of making faster motors," he says. "One year in the early 1970's L.J. Dennis went through 26 motors. He has been the area's best driver, and the most active in racing."

When I asked Dick Rugh why he has spent his life dedicated to racing, helping others race, and making faster motors, he leaned back, "It's like drugs, the desire for the sound of racing motors, and the smell of oil. It's being able to do something someone else can't do. I consider myself a racer's friend. Fifty percent of my life revolves around racing."

Left: Larry Baker's first race car. Right: Baker's second car. His uncle, Fred Johnson was #56.

Larry Baker, new paint job.

Speedway Kings, 1980 – 2011

And then a young Steve Baker gave them a run for their money.

Randy Combs wins big at the Hagerstown Speedway, July 2, 1982. Mark Richards, right with trophy. Josh Richards holds the checkered flag, something he has enjoyed in his own racing career.

In 1986, Mark Richards and Steve Baker began building chasis in Mark's father's garage. "You can't make a living with racing," Dad told them. By 1991, Rocket Chasis was becoming well known. When I asked Steve how many they had built so far, he knew the number, 3,682. They were shipping one to Australia at that moment.

Baker grew up at the Morgantown Speedway as his parents helped run the show. I asked Jean Baker how old Steve was when he first visited the track. "Almost two weeks old," she said.

"It's been my whole life," he smiled, sitting back reminiscing.

Steve Baker and Mark Richards are unassuming, but their Rocket Chasis operation is top-notch. "Rockets around the world," Mark laughed. His son, Josh Richards, is 2009 and 2010 World of Outlaws Late Model Series Champion. In the photo below, you are seeing Josh behind the wheel of a race car for the first time. His cousin, Frank Baker (Steve's son), cheers him on. They look so happy! Their parents also ran the I 79 Interstate Speedway from 1998 – 2003.

Arsenberger Trucking race car #26, Mill Run, 1986.

Bobby Henry, June 1987, Motordrome.

Dirt Henry, 1988. Connellsville Senior High School is in the background. Dirt said that he asked his wife one day, who is wise with a penny, why she let him spend so much money on race cars for their boys. She said that this allowed her to always know where they were and what they were doing.

"If I can hear them down there working on their cars, I know they are not out getting in trouble," she told her husband of many decades.

When I asked Dirt why he did it, he smiled. "If I could have the money back that I spent on racing for over fifty years," he looked at me, laughing, "I'd do it again."

Bobby Henry, 1989. Bobby, Dirt's youngest son, is still winning today.

Jimmy "Bender" Bendishaw, Sr. wins the Pure Stock feature in
his #41 "Mongoose, Bad to the Bone" at Motordrome, 1984.

My one regret about publishing this book is that Jimmy is not here to be interviewed for it and to enjoy telling his stories. Bender raced on in 2007, but before he did, I had many years of knowing him, as he was married to my best friend, Pam Lambi Bendishaw, twice. The second time I performed the ceremony myself. The three of us had been through a lot together by then. Kids, Jimmy getting burned racing, divorces, and life.

At several of my interviews this summer, Jimmy's friends and family made reference to their rough and tumble friend. Pam Bendishaw said very simply and to the point, "He had a need for speed." This could not be more true, and it is very evidently in the blood of his sons and grandsons.

"Jimmy always took credit for my staying in school. One day I skipped classes and went to his house. He was working on a car. I stayed there all day helping him work on that motor. I thought I would freeze to death. I never skipped school again," laughed Garry Sisson.

Danna Whipkey, Jimmy's daughter, said, "When we were little and Dad went to work, Mom had to keep an oily rag on her shoulder. If she didn't, Jimmy, Jr. would be upset all day."

Dick Rugh, "Jimmy was a tough driver. He and L.J. were always neck and neck, it seemed. Young Jimmy is the best today. No one can maneuver a car on the track like Jimmy Bendishaw."

I have a few Bender stories, but will only share this one. A few of you have heard it. I know I told it after his wake. Jimmy and I went to the Goodwill Auto Auctions for a few years in the late 1990's, and early 2000's. We were there on September 11th all those years ago. One Tuesday morning we rode together with my friend, Mark. Jimmy bought a Crown Victoria that he had a customer for. I bought a $50. Ford Tempo with a blown motor. My twin daughters had been through a car or two by then, and my sister had a motor to donate for this car.

Instead of calling Jimmy, Jr. to tow the Tempo, Jimmy said to me, "Yours has enough juice left to make it if you give me a tap once in a while. I will signal you if I need you to give me a nudge."

Mark looked at me like we were both mad, but I laughed and said, "Okay."

The auction was and is in Irwin. We were heading to Bender's in Uniontown. I gave him the occasional push when he waved at me, but when we got out of the cars in Uniontown he grabbed his neck and laughed, "I said to tap me, but geez!"

Mark shook his head, mumbling something about the Clampetts.

Kenny Mitchell grew up next to the old board track property. He said that when they were young they had a huge shed made of the wood from the track. It was also filled with boards from the famous track. He said the boards were grooved so they fit snugly together.

When I sat down with Kenny and asked him what his funniest Bender story was, he said, "I went to the races with Jimmy a lot. This was more funny to him." I laughed. "We were late for the races one night at Interstate 79. That's when he was hauling on that open trailer with the old Suburban."

I remembered, shaking my head. "Well, he was in a hurry and passed everyone on the road, then traffic was at a stop on I 79. He looked at me and said, 'We're gonna be late.' As he said that, he pulled up on the median. We drove the median for eleven miles and never got stopped. We were flying with that old open trailer loaded. We were not late. He was unreal."

In the late 1990's, Ken Schrader came to the I 79 Interstate Speedway in Shinston, West Virginia.

Bob Arsenberger's first asphalt win, Jennerstown, 1990.

Rocket on the wall at Cherokee Speedway, 1996. Tim Hitt, Driver. It does say "Rocket" on it!

Bob Arsenberger at Jennerstown Speedway, 1996.

Bob Arsenberger thanks his crew for their years of dedication, and although Steve Brooks is not in this photo, Bob said that without Brooks, he could not have had as many wins with his asphalt cars.

Mark Bigam, Wilmer Miller, Bobby Ainsley, Bob Arsenberger, and John Schokey. Tom Clark 150, Motordrome Speedway, July 7, 2000. (Bill Sherman Photos)

In the year 2000, Jimmy and Pam Bendishaw opened Bender's Pit Stop. Many a Roaring Knob race car driver and friend gave their photos as gifts to them for the grand opening. Here are a few...

Jimmy Shaffer of Shaffer Towing in Masontown, PA.

Bobby Lake Motorsports car, driven by Mike Benedum. Lake has crewed, driven and owned cars over the 35 span of his racing career. Today he also sponsors his young grandson, Michael, who has 5 track champs and a "Love for speed."

"Just keep racing," Bobby Lake.

Mel Minnick, Jr., Roaring Knob, 2000. "I felt the power the first time I drove. I was born to drive," Mel said when I asked him how it all started for him. He worked in his dad's garage driving the tow truck before it was legal for him to do so. His father rigged his license so Mel, Jr. could take those late night calls. "I finally got my real birth year on my license this year," He chuckled.

Bob Nelson #99, Roaring Knob Motorsports Complex.

Notice that Jim Bendishaw, left, now has L. J. Dennis' (right with checkered flag) lucky #7. Those who have known these men and watched them drive through the years will tell you that they have put on many an exciting show. Far right: Jim Murchot, who owned the track during this period. Bender had number 33, 34, and 41, the "Mongoose, Bad to the Bone," among other numbers.

Pittsburgh's Pennsylvania Motor Speedway, Sept. 17, 2000. L – R: Josh Richards, Joe Paxon, Davie Johnson (driver), Anthony Tomaro, Tania and Danny Smith. The Smiths are Rocket Chasis dealers in Australia. They spent many summers traveling and helping to crew chief for Rocket Chasis. (Rick Schwallie Photos)

Left: Bobby Henry, 2003. Right: Bob Arsenberger's last race car, 2004. It lasted him 5 years, unlike some cars in the past! When I asked Bob why he went through so many cars, his wife laughed. I think racing wives have extraordinary senses of humor!

Garry Sisson (center with checkered flag) wants to thank his family and team for their years of support. This is a feature win at Roaring Knob, 2005.

Garry would especially like to thank Pee Wee George for being a faithful crew chief, (below left with trophy) for Sisson's entire racing career. Pee Wee said, when I asked, "I enjoyed my many years with him. We almost had three in a row in 2007, but did he tell you the principal took his coil wire?"

Garry wants to make a special dedication to Jim Silbaugh (center) and Red Christopher (right).

Josh Bendishaw takes the checkers at Roaring Knob, June 16, 2007, the day he buried his father, Jimmy Bendishaw, Sr. Jimmy Bendishaw, Jr., rides in passenger seat. Jimmy Jr.'s son, James Bendishaw, carries the American flag. Josh Bendishaw #33. 6th Place Points Finish. 616 Points. 9 Top 5's, 11 Top Ten's, 15 Starts, 2 Heat Race Wins. GNH Trucking Street Stocks. 2007

When I interviewed Josh and Jimmy Jr. for this book, it was a treat. Although I have known them for 25 years, I have never had a time where they were both sitting across the booth from me talking about their father and racing. The differences in the men are evident. Jimmy tells a story at a measured pace, like Jimmy, Sr., pausing for effect while those big brown eyes laugh.
Josh's demeanor is restless and observant like his mom. Several of his stories ended with a look at his brother and these words, "and then he beat me."

Jimmy Jr. had a great year at the track this season, but after our chat he took me aside saying, "You know that as soon as Josh's mind catches up with his foot, I am in trouble." He said this with pride and humor, just like Josh said, "and then he beat me." All Jimmy's sons and grand sons seem to have inherited his "need for speed." James is out in California breaking into films as a stunt man. Can you guess what he is working on as a specialty? Yes, that's right, driving the high speed chases in action films. What else?

Josh's son, Bryce, graduated from pre-school in June. During the celebration, his teachers told what they felt each child was destined to become. When it came to Bryce they said, "Race car driver."

"In Memory of Jim Bendishaw, 1944 – 2007. L – R: Garry Sisson, Patty Leighgabor, Chance Leighgabor, Danna and Brian Whipkey, Tina Bendishaw, Jimmy Bendishaw, Jr. with daughter, Sophia, on shoulders. Mel Minnick, Jr. in red driver's suit, Pam Bendishaw with hand on door. Kneeling to the left are James and Maddie Bendisahaw, and Johnny Thorpe. Linda Lewis flanks James' left shoulder, Brooke Sandusky is behind the other.

Standing to the right is Josh Bendishaw holding baby Bryce, Kristen Beatty with hand on shoulder of Brandy Bendishaw, Jade Bendishaw, Bill Bendishaw, and Paula Lambi. Jolene Bendishaw is in front of Jade. Tanner and Tucker Pritts are kneeling. A heartbreaking evening at Roaring Knob, June 16, 2007.

Mel Minnick makes a one-wheel-pass at Roaring Knob Motorsports Complex, 2010. This veteran sold his car this year. Years ago his dog died and he made a roll cage out of his pen. I am just saying, "Stay tuned."

Mason Zeigler takes the checkered flag at Roaring Knob on August, 20, 2011, his 18th birthday. His father, Fred Zeigler, is second from right. Thanks, crew! Four years earlier, when Mason began driving, I was at the races. Afterwards I said, "Mason, it is hard for me to watch you go that fast. How do you do it?" I will always remember his look when he said, "Balls to the wall."

Geico Crew member (left) and Mason Zeigler (right) were invited this past year by Head Pit crew man Aaron Pieratt to come and join them in the pits in Miami, Florida. Mason worked the Geico team and Dan worked the Aaron's rental team. Aaron Pieatt had the fastest pit crew of the Daytona Races.

Photo by Cauldwell/Counts Photography

Stacey Bortz, Farmington, PA, sells insurance…and goes up to 145mph on her Harley.! Around 2006 she bought her third motorcycle (a Super Glide she still owns). She was just beginning to appreciate and understand horsepower and sought more of the motorcycle experience besides the leisurely riding she was accustomed to.

After having gone to the drag strip a couple of times with Gregg Dahl, saw him teaching a couple of his friends to race alongside him. The realization that she could do that, too, changed her life. Today she is the only lady riding a street legal Harley with no wheelie bars to do the ¼ drag strip at 145mph. Bortz races with the American Motorcycle Racing Association. "I don't think it is possible to describe to describe the sense of accomplishment and personal reward that racing gives me." This 2011 season, she took national runner up for the Hot Street class, and reset a Hot Street speed record of 122.23 mph in the 1/8 mile.

Photo by Cauldwell/Counts Photography

Gregg Dahl drag racing his 1985 highly modified Harley Super Glide. Dahl grew up hearing about the old board track, and learning from Uniontown's old timers in the garages around town. His father has always owned very old cars and although Dahl has had other jobs, his owning GMS Racing Engines in Uniontown is no surprise. It used to be that boys learned to drive most anything with wheels almost from birth. Many of the men in this book will tell you that they could drive at a very early age. Some like four wheels, some two. Dahl specializes in motorcycles both in business and recreation. He races with the American Motorcycle Racing Association in the Outlaw class.

"Ernie Cerini was my first sponsor for the drag races. It really takes a team to show up with the best bike by race day.

The associations and friends you meet bring in a lot of business. There are few "hobbies" that are this much hard work and that require so many skills. Engineering, fundraising, focus, and the need for speed.

I am interested in the board tracks because they were the stadiums of the day. All automotive advancements were developed for the boards. Chevrolet pioneered all the engineering used today. It was complete hard work and intelligence. They were heroes and gentlemen. The Industrial Revolution started everything. They accelerated advancements in automotive technology by 50 years by racing on boards."

"They used long stroke engines to get their power displacement. Bored motors out of metal."

"Those cars sounded like tractors going 100mph on wood!"

Speedy Lane leads to GMS Motors which is in one of the old garages from the board track days, and sits just behind Charlie Johnson's old Standard Garage. Speedy Lane has seen a lot of horsepower.

Marci McGuinness (right) would like to thank Ed Cope (left) for his support through the decades.

Author, Publisher, Marci Lynn McGuinness brings you her 26th book, *Speedway Kings of Southwestern Pennsylvania & Region*, 100 Years of Racing History, in celebration of her 30th year in book publishing. McGuinness is presently working to produce both a documentary and a feature film about the story behind the Uniontown Speedway board track. Be sure to collect all her Speedway publications including *Yesteryear at the Uniontown Speedway* and the reprint of the 68-page program from the 1916 Uniontown Speedway Preliminary Race.

Many of McGuinness' books concern the area's history. Here is a list of the prolific author's available books (www.ohiopyle.info; www.uniontownspeedway.com).

Yesteryear at the Uniontown Speedway (1996, 2nd Edition 1997, 3rd Edition 2008)
Official Program U.S.A. Speedway, 1916 Reprint (1996, 2nd Edition 2009)
Message of the Sacred Buffalo (June 2010)
Hauntings of Pittsburgh & the Laurel Highlands (October 2009)
Gone to Ohiopyle (September 2009)
Murder in Ohiopyle & Other Incidents (Summer 2009)
Butch's Smack Your Lips BBQ Cookbook, (Spring 2009)
Yesteryear in Ohiopyle and Surrounding Communities, Volume III (2008)
The Explorer's Guide to the Youghiogheny River, Ohiopyle and SW PA Villages (2000)
Along the Baltimore & Ohio Railroad, from Cumberland to Uniontown (1998)
Stone House Legends & Lore (1998)
Yesteryear in Smithfield (1996)
Yesteryear in Masontown (1994)
Yesteryear in Ohiopyle and Surrounding Communities, Volume II (1994)
Yesteryear in Ohiopyle and Surrounding Communities, Volume I (1993)

Contact the author: shorepublications@yahoo.com; 724-710-2919

A-CEE'S
Car Care
724-437-1601
FREE Pick Up & Delivery

WASH - INSIDE & OUT
WASH, WAX & BUFF
INTERIOR SHAMPOO
ENGINE STEAM CLEAN
PA STATE INSPECTION
OIL CHANGE
BRAKES & ROTORS
MINOR REPAIRS

OWNER – ANTHONY CAROLLA
OVER 24 YEARS IN BUSINESS

410 W. Main Street, Masontown, PA 15461

Tilt Bed Towing   Buying Junk & Unwanted Cars
State Inspection   Auto Repairs

724-583-0811   After 5: 724-583-0338

Uniontown, Pennsylvania

HENRY MOTOR SALES

Since 1956, Dirt Henry has sold over 10,000 cars at
800 Snyder Street, Connellsville, PA.

He is "Super Ornery" and a fair and honest man,
bringing him generations of customers from area families.

"Everyone Drives a Used Car."   **724-628-1432**

ANSEL'S TIRE OUTLET, INC.

Lewis O. Ansel, Sr., 1963
1946 Harley Davidson Bobber

Family-owned and serving the area since 1935.

1708 MCCLELLANDTOWN ROAD, MCCLELLANDTOWN, PA 15458   724-737-5556

Made in United States
Cleveland, OH
05 November 2024

10474222R00074